Notebook Covers and More

COMPILED BY **Lindsey Murray McClelland**

INTERWEAVE.
interweave.com

Interweave grants permission to
photocopy the templates in this
publication for personal use.

*The projects in this collection were
originally published in other Interweave
publications, including* 101 Patchwork,
Modern Patchwork, Quilt Scene,
Quilting Arts, *and* Stitch *magazines
and 'QATV.' Some have been altered to
update information and/or conform to
space limitations.*

Interweave Press LLC
A division of F+W Media, Inc
201 East Fourth Street
Loveland, CO 80537
interweave.com

Manufactured in the United States
by Versa Press

ISBN 978-1-59668-766-0 (pbk.)

Table of Contents

Vintage Quilt Covers
by Pat Schuman

For years I've collected antique quilts. While I cherish the
ones that are in good condition, I especially enjoy giving new
life to old quilts that are worn from years of use and love.
I cut them up, preserving the portions that are still intact,
and use them to make one-of-a-kind gifts: lampshades,
stuffed animals, and much more. These book covers are just
one of the ways to bring new life to an old treasure.

Materials

—Piece of a worn-out antique quilt
  (You'll need a rectangle slightly larger
  than the book to be covered.)

—Muslin

—Book (to cover)

—Sewing machine

—Thread

Directions

1 Measure the height and the entire
width (width of the top, plus the
spine width, plus the width of the
back) of the book you wish to cover.

2 Add 1" (2.5 cm) to the height and
width dimensions, and cut the
piece of antique quilt to this size. Set
aside.

3 Cut 2 muslin rectangles as follows.
The height should be 1" (2.5 cm)
greater than the height of your book.
The width should be 1" (2.5 cm) less
than the width of the front cover of
your book.

4 Hem each muslin rectangle along
one long side. To do this, turn
the raw edge under ¼" (6 mm) and
press. Fold again and press, and then
topstitch ⅛" (3 mm) from the fold.

5 Place the quilt rectangle
right-side up on your work
surface. Layer a muslin rectangle on

each end, wrong-side up, aligning the muslin raw edges with the quilt raw edges. Pin to hold in place.

6 Using a ¼" (6 mm) seam allowance, stitch along the raw edges of the muslin rectangles to secure them to the quilt.

7 Clip the corners and turn the book cover right-side out.

8 To finish, turn the exposed raw quilt edge ¼" (6 mm) to the wrong side and topstitch ⅛" (3 mm) from the fold. Repeat for the opposite edge.

Slip your book inside the cover and enjoy! 🍃

PAT SCHUMAN began selling items made from antique quilts and other vintage fabrics in 1984. She now vends mainly at quilt shows and antique shows.

Journal Cover

WITH ZIPPER POCKET

by Valori Wells

A handmade fabric cover adds a delightful touch to an everyday journal, and this cover goes one step further: it includes a zippered pocket for convenient storage of your journaling tools. Now you'll never be without your favorite pencils! For the exterior of my journal cover, I used a piece of home-dec weight screen-printed fabric; the lining is a bright floral print from my "Wrenly" fabric collection with FreeSpirit.

Materials

—Fits a 5½" × 8½" (14 × 21.5 cm) journal

—Fabric for exterior: 1 rectangle 10" × 15" (25.5 × 38 cm), 1 rectangle 3" × 10" (7.5 × 25.5 cm)

—Fabric for lining, 1 rectangle 10" × 18½" (25.5 × 47 cm)

—Fabric for pocket, 2 rectangles 4½" × 10" (11.5 × 25.5 cm; I used the same fabric as the lining.)

—Interfacing (mid-weight, fusible on one side), 1 rectangle 10" × 15" (25.5 × 38 cm), 1 rectangle 3" × 10" (7.5 × 25.5 cm)

—7" (18 cm) zipper

—5½" × 8½" (14 × 21.5 cm) journal

---

note

* Use ¼" (6 mm) seams throughout. These instructions will lead you to make a cover to fit a 5½" × 8½" (14 × 21.5 cm) journal. If you wish to make a cover for a different-sized journal, adjust the measurements as needed.

Directions

1 Fuse the interfacing rectangles to the wrong side of the same-sized exterior fabric rectangles.

2 Layer the large interfaced exterior fabric rectangle (right-side up), the zipped zipper (right-side down and centered along a 10" [25.5 cm] edge), and 1 pocket rectangle (right-side down and aligned along the same edge). Pin. Using a zipper foot and a ⅜" (1 cm) seam allowance, stitch the layers together.

3 Open the piece and press both fabrics away from the zipper teeth (so the wrong sides of the fabrics are together). With the exterior fabric faceup, edgestitch along the zipper.

4 In the same manner, layer, pin, and sew the remaining exterior fabric rectangle and pocket rectangle to the other side of the zipper. Press and edgestitch.

5 Match the pocket fabrics so the right sides are together. Stitch around the 3 open edges of the pocket to close it.

6 Place the exterior fabric rectangle flat on your work surface,

right-side up, with the zipper and narrow exterior fabric strip all placed out flat and right-side up. The pocket will be underneath; position it so it's under the large rectangle.

7 Layer the lining fabric rectangle on the front fabric, right sides together; trim the lining if necessary. Stitch around all 4 edges, leaving an opening for turning along 1 long side. Clip the corners and turn the piece right-side out through the opening. Turn the seam allowance along the opening to the inside; press.

8 Topstitch the short sides only.

9 To create the flaps, fold 2½" (6.5 cm) to the lining side at each end and pin to hold (the zipper should be along the fold of 1 flap). To secure the zipper fold, topstitch from the top of the piece just down to the top of the zipper, backtacking at both ends. Do the same at the bottom of the zipper.

10 Topstitch along the top and bottom edges of the cover, securing the flaps in the seam and being sure to catch the unstitched seam allowance of the opening used for turning the piece.

11 Insert your journal and your writing/drawing tools and enjoy! ✿

Find **VALORI WELLS** online at valoriwells.com.

Materials

—Sketchbook, photo album, or other book that you wish to cover

—Fabric (I prefer plain black) for the inside cover

—Batting (or stabilizer, such as interfacing or muslin)

—Fabric scraps

Optional

—Fusible web

—Paint, stencils, stamps, and other surface design supplies

—Beads, mostly seed and smaller or flat beads

—Beading thread (I use Silamide or Nymo.)

—Appliqué needles (Beading needles bend too easily for my taste.)

—Aleene's Jewel-It or E-6000

Directions

1 Choose your book and lay it (closed) on your batting. Use a marker to trace around the book's cover. Without picking up the book, turn it onto its spine, trace that, then turn it onto its other cover, marking the outline.

2 Cut your batting or stabilizer to size, leaving an extra ½" (1.3 cm) around each side for a seam allowance.

Note: As you think about your design, remember that it will have three parts: the front cover, the spine, and the back cover.

3 If you choose to sew, grab your scrap bag and piece fabrics together until you have a piece large enough to cover the batting. Baste or fuse your fabric piece to your batting or stabilizer.

Tip

If you choose to fuse, adhere your favorite fusible web onto the back side of your fabric scraps then peel the paper off. Your scissors will thank you later.

Artful Book Covers
by Lyric Kinard

If you've ever wondered what gift to give to another artist, here is the perfect idea. How about the gift of your own artwork, covering a new sketchbook or photo album? It can be put together quickly, and can be as simple or complex as your time and creativity allow. I have also enjoyed doing this project with children, covering a notebook or journal for a special event, such as a summer vacation or birthday. It doesn't take much in the way of materials and can also be one of those "keep your hands busy" take-along projects, small enough to fit in your purse.

4 If you are fusing, cut, collage, then adhere your designs to the background fabric. You can now fuse your composition to the batting or stabilizer.

Once you have a fabric design large enough to cover the batting you may choose to skip straight to construction of the book cover or add surface design, stitching, or embellishments.

Note: Keep in mind that the viewer will usually only see one cover at a time, and that the spine area will receive a lot of wear.

Surface design

5 Pull out your stencils, stamps, brushes, and screens, and apply paint to your design. I love to mask out part of the design with freezer paper and then sponge paint through the plastic mesh that comes on my tangerine boxes for a lovely lizard-skin effect.

6 Use paint sticks, foil, photo transfer, or other techniques . . . this is the perfect time to try something new. Try using cut vegetables (celery, onion, peppers) to stamp designs for the cover of a vegetarian cookbook for your favorite foodie! Let the veggies sit, cut-side down, on a paper towel for a few minutes first. This helps the surfaces dry off enough for the paint to stick.

7 Skip to construction or add more texture with stitching and embellishment.

Embellishing

8 Pull out your fancy metallic thread and stitch a grid of straight lines or whatever you think might add to the success of your design. This project is a perfect size to test out and refine your free-motion quilting skills.

9 Try some subtle colors for echo-quilting around main design elements, or be bold and use stitch and embroidery threads themselves as the main element of your design.

10 Add beads, charms, fringe . . . any embellishment that suits your fancy. Keep in mind: a book cover will get much more wear than an art quilt. Sew down every bead with at least twice as many passes of thread as you normally would, especially along the spine. Also, remember that books often get piled on top of each other. Save bulky beads or dangles for the spines of the book where they won't get in the way or catch onthings.

> **Tip**
>
> If you are pressed for time or don't like hand sewing, I have found that both Gem-Tac and Aleene's Jewel-It are very strong adhesives for adding beads to fabric.

Finishing

11 Cut the inside cover fabric to the same size as your batting and then cut this piece down the center (where the spine is marked) and fold back the inside edges.

12 Measure and cut a strip of fabric 4" (10 cm) wider than the spine.

13 Layer your cover, backing, and spine cover, according to the illustration below.

14 Lay your book out as in the very first step and recheck your dimensions, redrawing your outlines if necessary.

15 Pin the layers together, right sides together; pin carefully around the spine cover.

> **Tip**
>
> I find that taking two stitches diagonally across each corner, instead of making a 90-degree turn, will help your corners turn cleanly.

16 Sew completely around the outside edges. (If you've added beads, use a zipper foot.)

17 Trim your seam allowances and corners, and turn the book cover right-side out. Roll the seams between your fingers until they are straight and fully open. Gently open your book inside out, until the covers are almost touching each other, and insert the book's covers into the sleeves. Gently work them all the way in until you can close your book. ✐

LYRIC KINARD creates award-winning wall quilts and wearable works of art. To see more of her work, visit lyrickinard.com.

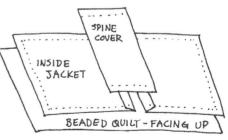

SPINE COVER

INSIDE JACKET

BEADED QUILT - FACING UP

Winter Journal Cover
by Lucie Summers

These covered journals are really easy and fun to make and look terrific using original, printed fabrics. I first started making these, using diaries, as Christmas gifts a few years ago. They were a huge success and greatly appreciated by the recipients. Since then, I've refined the design to make it simpler to put together. These journals would be particularly suitable as holiday gifts, especially for artistic friends, or as diaries for those without a creative streak. Although these journals have a holiday feel, they make lovely presents for lots of other occasions. Other possibilities include covering small photograph albums for a baby's first Christmas, or using different stamps and inspiration for a couple celebrating their wedding.

Materials

— A plain sketchbook or notebook with good-quality paper, no larger than 8" × 8" (20.5 × 20.5 cm) (I use a brand called Seawhites.)

— Pieces of winter-inspired fabrics (commercial or hand-dyed), at least 1" (2.5 cm) longer than your book and 4"–5" (10–12.5 cm) wide

— 3 or 4 used Shout Color Catcher sheets (see page 12)

— A piece of fine felt, 6" (15 cm) longer than the width (including the spine) and ¼" (6 mm) longer than the height of your book

— Sewing machine with a walking foot

— Thread in several colors to match your fabrics

— Spray glue or fusible glue

— A pair of pinking shears or a wavy blade rotary cutter

— Strong textile glue (I use waterproof PVA wood glue.)

— Embellishments such as beads, sequins, shaped paper punches, brass paper fasteners, brads, eyelets, scraps of interesting paper, ribbons, lace, embossing pads and powder, paper tags, scraps of leather

— Winter or holiday-inspired "focal point" stamps

— 2 or 3 general background stamps, such as spots and dots, stripes, and diamonds

— Acrylic craft paint in a number of colors, metallic and non-metallic

— Foam rollers: 2" (5 cm) wide are perfect for this project

Optional
— A piece of thin ribbon, if you want to have a bookmark.

Directions

To make the journal cover

1 Open the book and center it on the precut piece of felt. (Allow an extra 3" [7.5 cm] on either end and ⅛" [3 mm] on the top and bottom.) Mark the book flaps by tracing along the edges of the book. Transfer these markings onto the other side of the felt. This will be your guide for folding the book flaps.

2 Arrange your fabrics and/or Color Catchers over the felt. You can cut the pieces down to make more of a

patchwork effect or leave the pieces whole—this is what I tend to do. Slightly overlap the fabrics so the felt doesn't show. It is a good idea to keep folding the piece of felt in half just to see what the front will look like when the piece is wrapped around the book; this way it can be easily changed if something doesn't work. The fabrics should extend at least 1" (2.5 cm) beyond the outer edges, all the way around. When you are happy with the arrangement, glue the fabrics in place.

3 Using a walking foot on your machine, zigzag over the raw edges. Use a thread that blends nicely with your fabrics, and remember, if you don't want your stitches to show on the back of the cover, match your thread to the color of the felt.

4 Change the thread color and quilt with a straight stitch over the entire piece, changing thread colors as you wish. I usually quilt a random grid over the cover. You can, of course, quilt any design you wish.

5 Trim the excess around the edges down to around ½" (1.3 cm). On the 2 short sides a straight blade is fine, but on the longer sides use pinking shears or a rotary cutter with a wavy blade. This is just to make it look nice on the inside of the cover.

6 Turn over the edges of the 2 short sides and iron. Pin in place and stitch down, using a ¼" (6 mm) seam.

7 Turn over the edges of the 2 long sides and iron. Use a glue stick to keep the edge down, not pins. If you want to have a ribbon bookmark, pin this exactly in the middle of the top edge—make sure that this is in the middle of the spine.

8 Fold over the flaps and pin very close to the edge. Check that the cover fits the book. This rarely fits the first time around and it will probably need a bit of adjustment. The trick is to get it to fit snugly, but not too tightly. Remember to keep checking that the flaps are still equal widths.

9 Stitch as close as you can to the folded edge (a touch less than ⅛" [3 mm]), and stitch slowly. There is quite a lot of bulk to stitch through, but be patient and it will go together with no problems at all. Check that the book fits correctly.

10 Tie the loose threads at each corner and stitch to secure.

11 Take out the book and embellish the cover as you desire. This is where you can really let your imagination go wild—use beads, sequins, glitter glue, and charms to personalize your book cover. Remember to stitch each item down securely: if the book is going to be used frequently, or kept in a handbag, it needs to be able to stand up to a bit of wear and tear.

Tips for embellishment

12 The background stars on the "Wintergreen" journal were made by using a paper punch to cut shaped pieces of thin leather. I glued them onto the front using strong textile glue. I stitched green star sequins on top of the leather and finished them off by tying on a bronze bead and leaving strands of the green thread on for show.

13 The holly motif on the black-and-gray "First Frost" journal was created using a clear embossing pad and black sparkle embossing powder. On fabric, the powder doesn't raise but does give a nice bit of glitz. For a raised effect, do the same thing on a thick watercolor paper and attach by handstitching through the paper. Add beads or sequins as desired.

14 On the pink "Partridge and Pear" journal, I painted the paper tags in bronze acrylic, stamped out a large circle shape, and then placed scraps of sheet music behind the "window." I stuck these down with strong textile glue, then attached a small chrome-colored paper fastener through the hole where the string usually goes. I then stitched through the tags for extra security.

15 On the small "Ice Blue" journal I added a small tree in white onto a piece of screen-printed linen, naively stitched in white along the top and bottom, and then added small, silver seed beads. I applied a row of bugle beads and finally stitched a row of crosses along the bottom section of plain, blue linen.

Ideas for book closures

I generally like to leave the book without any aid to keep it closed, like the "Wintergreen" journal, but I had a lot of fun playing around with some ideas.

16 The pink "Partridge and Pear" journal closure is simply a piece of 1" (2.5 cm) wide organza ribbon, stitched in the middle of the spine and tied at the edges. I think this would be lovely as a gift to a bride or bridesmaid, especially with a photograph album to record the special day. It would be particularly lovely if created using pieces of fabrics from the dresses. Choose a ribbon you can see through so it doesn't spoil any other focal point on the cover.

17 The "Ice Blue" journal closure was made using a piece of strong cord. This was threaded through the crease in the book flap, using a large needle, and knotted. On the other end of the cord I tied a small single-hole button. The knot was dabbed with PVA glue and left to dry. I stitched a larger mother-of-pearl button 1" (2.5 cm) away from the edge of the book and wrapped the cord around the button to close the book. The little button acts as a tab.

18 With the black-and-gray "First Frost" journal, I used a piece of thin gray ribbon as a closure. A piece was threaded through both book flap creases and the ends knotted. For extra decoration I used 2 small, single-hole buttons, threaded them onto the ribbon, and tied a knot to keep them in place. The ends of the ribbon were sealed with a candle flame and then tied in a bow.

The finishing touch

If you are making a journal for a gift, think about adding the recipient's initials or a word ("peace" or "joy" would be lovely) by embossing them using puff paint. Spread a little of the puff paint over a piece of fabric or paper, then stamp or write the initials or word firmly into the wet surface. Dry, using a heat gun, and rub a little metallic paint into the raised surface. Cut out the initials or word, leaving a border of around ½" (1.3 cm), and handstitch into place on the cover.

To make your journal even more special, make a label from card stock or fabric with your name on it and stitch it somewhere on the journal. I use a computer and change the font on every letter, and stitch it in by hand. If it is for a gift, you could write a special message too. I like to put mine on the front book flap so everyone can see it when the book is opened. 🖋

Visit **LUCIE SUMMERS** online at atsummersville.etsy.com.

Color Catchers

Shout Color Catcher is a product designed to catch the loose dye in the washing machine while washing your clothes. It comes in small white sheets (around 5" × 10" [12.5 × 25.5 cm]) of what I call a "paper fiber"—they can withstand being wet like fabric, but they rip like paper, and don't fray. My mum began using them some time ago in her washing machine and we both began to get interested in what color they came out as—mainly various tones of gray. It was only when she put one in with a new pair of dark denim jeans that we both realized the potential for these gems. The sheet came out a gorgeous shade of blue, just right for a project I was working on.

Since then, I have been collecting mountains of these sheets and squirreling them away. I discovered that they take dye and paint beautifully (which of course is what they're for) and are perfect for making these journal covers. They can be used straight from the washing machine (but quite often they come out gray from a colored wash—you can paint dye over a pale one to give a different base color) or you can decorate them with acrylic paints and fabric dyes. Heavily painted Color Catchers feel gorgeous, almost like leather or suede. Another advantage they have over fabric is that they can be used with paper punches, which look great as embellishments. The following instructions are for decorating Color Catchers, but you can obviously use fabric instead.

Painting the fabric

1 Decide on your color palette. For "First Frost," the small, black-and-white journal, I used metallic graphite, silver, white, black, and gray.

2 Roll a layer of metallic paint over the fabric or Color Catcher and either leave it to dry or iron it dry. (If you decide to do this, use a piece of scrap paper or paper towel to protect your iron.)

3 Wash a darker color over the whole piece, leaving some areas of the original color showing.

4 Roll on a very fine layer of a pale color.

5 Using silver acrylic and a general background stamp, randomly stamp over the fabric.

6 Stamp a more prominent focal point stamp in a stronger, more contrasting color.

7 Do the same to the other Color Catchers or fabrics, but vary the tones; make one overall very pale with a hint of darker color; make another more medium in tone. Try to use similar stamps in all of them, so there is a link between all of the pieces. It is also nice to have one with lots of texture but no stamping and to mix and match Color Catchers with other fabrics (cotton, linen, and silk are great) for your journal because it is visually interesting to have contrasts in texture.

Materials
— Featured fabric (for front/back)

— Lining fabric

— Canvas for the spine (or use fabric that has been reinforced with a layer of interfacing)

— Accent fabric (for the inner flaps)

— Pre-fused accent fabric (for the stitched motif background)

— Mid-weight woven fusible interfacing

— Fusible batting

— ¼" (6 mm) elastic (flat-braided or wrapped), 12" (30.5 cm) length (for a 9" [23 cm] tall journal)

— Neutral color sewing thread

— Heavy cotton decorative variegated thread

— New denim/topstitch needle

---

note

✳ All seam allowances are ½" (1.3 cm).

Directions

These instructions will allow you to make a custom-sized cover for your favorite journal or sketchbook. You'll want to add your own touches to your cover, depending on the journal size you are working with. For example, smaller journals may look better with a simple loop of ribbon or fabric near the top to hold your pen, and the smallest journals won't have room for either the pen holder or the internal pockets.

Measure, cut, and interface

1 Record the measurements of your journal in the chart on the next page (we've gotten you started if you're using a 6" × 9" × 1¼" [15 × 23 × 3.2 cm] journal; otherwise you'll need to fill in the chart with your journal measurements). There is a tiny bit of math involved, but it makes this pattern much more useful!

Note: The total width (T) is best taken with a fabric measuring tape. To measure, begin on the front side edge of the journal and wrap it all the way around to the back side edge, making sure to include any binding (such as coils on the journal spine).

Journal & Sketchbook Cover
by Candy Glendening

I designed this pattern to feature a fabulous piece of fabric (hand-dyed or otherwise). A canvas spine protects the journal from wear and tear, and a slot for a pen or pencil is stitched into the seam. Elastic is sewn to the inside front cover, providing a way to hold the journal closed (or to mark a page). There is a business-card pocket on the inside front and a larger pocket on the inside back. Although this pattern works with any type of journal or sketch pad, I prefer to use ones that have stiff covers; they hold their shape better and are easier to use when there's not a table around.

FRONT COVER

Width (W)	Height (H)	Total Width (T)
6" (15 cm)	9" (23 cm)	13¼" (33.5 cm)

Fabric	Item	Fabric		Interfacing		Batting	
		Width	Height	Width	Height	Width	Height
Focus	Front & Back (2)	W + 1" (2.5 cm) 7" (18 cm)	H + 2" (5 cm) 11" (28 cm)	W + 1" 7" (18 cm)	H + 2" (5 cm) 11" (28 cm)	W − ¼" (6 mm) 5¾" (14.5 cm)	H + 1" (2.5 cm) 10" (25.5 cm)
Canvas	Spine	T − (2xW) + 2" (5 cm) 3¼" (8.5 cm)	H + 2" (5 cm) 11" (28 cm)	T − (2xW) + 2" 3¼" (8.5 cm)	H + 2" (5 cm) 11" (28 cm)	T − (2xW) + ¾" (2 cm) 2" (5 cm)	H + ¾" (2 cm) 9¾" (25 cm)
Lining	Inner Lining	T + 2" (5 cm) 15¼" (38.5 cm)	H + 2" (5 cm) 11" (28 cm)	T + 1" (2.5 cm) 14¼" (36 cm)	H + 1" (2.5 cm) 10" (25.5 cm)	**Note:** We filled in this chart (see the red entries) with measurements that are specific to a 6" × 9" (15 × 23 cm) journal with a 1¼" (3.2 cm) spine. If your journal is a different size, fill out the chart for your journal size (see "Directions").	
Accent	Inner Flaps (2)	W × 2 12" (30.5 cm)	H + 2" (5 cm) 11" (28 cm)	W − ½" (1.3 cm) 5½" (14 cm)	H + 1" (2.5 cm) 10" (25.5 cm)		
Lining	Business Card Holder	4" (10 cm)	6" (15 cm)	2½" (6.5 cm)	3" (7.5 cm)		
Lining	Back Pocket	W × 2 12" (30.5 cm)	H 9" (23 cm)	W − ½" (1.3 cm) 5½" (14 cm)	H − ½" (1.3 cm) 8½" (21.5 cm)		
Lining	Pen Holder	3" (7.5 cm)	7" (18 cm)	3" (7.5 cm)	5" (12.5 cm)		

2 Use a rotary cutter and ruler to cut out all the pieces. Label them with masking tape to keep them straight.

Note: Different pieces will be interfaced differently.

3 The front, back, and spine will become little mini quilts (the backing is interfacing rather than fabric). Lay the fabric pieces (right sides facing down) on your ironing board, center the batting, and then add the interfacing, fusible side down.

4 Using steam and a hot iron, fuse the sandwich together in a 3-step process (to avoid wrinkles around the perimeter): Start by lightly steaming and fuse-tacking the interfacing to the batting. Next, flip the sandwich over and press from the center out, fusing all three layers together. Flip it over again and give the edges an extra press to ensure that the interfacing

is well fused to the perimeter of the fabric (and the batting is safely enclosed in the middle).

5 Interface the inner lining piece by centering the interfacing (fusible side down) on the back of the lining; fuse. The lack of interfacing in the seam allowance will cut down on bulk.

6 To interface the inner flap rectangles and the business-card pocket fabric, fold each piece in half, wrong sides together, and press. Insert the interfacing into the fold, aligning the top of the interfacing with the top of the fold, and press.

7 To prepare the back pocket, fold the back pocket piece in half, wrong sides together (reducing the width), and press. Then fold the top corner down at a 45-degree angle and press (**figure 1**). Unfold and cut ½" (1.3 cm) above the fold, closer to

the top of the fabric (the fold line will become your stitching line) (**figure 2**). Fold the top corner of the back pocket interfacing down at a 45° angle, crease with your thumbnail, open up, and trim right on the line. Insert the interfacing into the folded pocket, aligning the side of the interfacing with the fold; the interfacing should be smaller than the fabric (**figure 3**).

8 Layer the pen holder fabric and interfacing; fuse. (The interfacing will extend to the edges on each side, but there will be a 1" [2.5 cm] margin of fabric at the top and bottom.)

9 Add decorative stitching to the outer panels as desired (see "Artify the Journal," above).

Prep the pockets

10 Fold the right sides of the business-card pocket together. Stitch around the sides and bottom

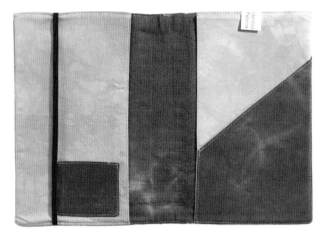

Journal cover interior (left) and exterior (right)

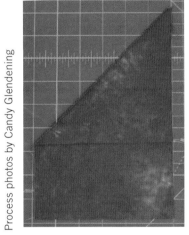

FIGURE 1

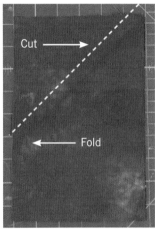

Cut

Fold

FIGURE 2

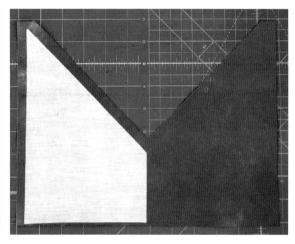

FIGURE 3

using the fused interfacing as a guide, leaving a 1" (2.5 cm) gap in the bottom for turning. Trim the corners, turn right-side out, press, and topstitch across the top folded edge. Topstitch the folded edge of the left front flap. Place the business-card pocket on the flap 1" (2.5 cm) up from the bottom raw edge and ½" (1.3 cm) in from the folded edge. Topstitch around the sides and bottom to attach the pocket, making sure to backstitch at the start and finish.

11 Fold the right sides of the back pocket together and stitch the angled seam. Trim the corner, turn right-side out, press, and topstitch only across the angled folded edge. Lay this pocket on top of the right flap, carefully aligning the folded edges of the flap and the pocket. (The raw edges of the bottoms will also align.) Starting at the bottom,

topstitch up the folded edge, securing the side of the pocket to the flap.

12 Fold the top and bottom seam allowances of the pen pocket in ½" (1.3 cm), and then another ½" (1.3 cm) (using the interfacing as a guide for the second fold), and press. Topstitch across the top. (I used a double seam, ⅛" [3 mm] and ⅜" [1 cm] down from the top.) Fold the pocket in half with the right sides facing out, press, and then topstitch across the bottom (again with a double seam, ⅛" [3 mm] and ⅜" [1 cm] up from the bottom).

Assembly

13 Aligning the raw edges and taking care to keep the bottom of the pen pocket at the bottom, place the pen pocket on the left edge of the journal front, 1½" (3.8 cm) up from the bottom. Place the spine on top of the front, with the right sides

How to Topstitch

Using a strong, sharp needle (denim or topstitch size 90/14 or 100/16), thick thread (I use a 24/3 ply), and a slightly longer stitch length (I use 1 click past the 3 mark on my Juki), stitch very close to the edge of the seam (I use a 2 cm edging foot).

together, and stitch. Open, and stitch
the back of the journal to the other
edge of the spine. Press the seams
open and topstitch along each side of
these two seams.

14 Place the lining right-side up.
Align the raw edges of the front
flap on the left side and the back flap
on the right side. Baste the flaps to
the lining. Baste your elastic about 2"
(5 cm) in from the left side.

Tip

When basting, I sew with a long
stitch length ¼" (6 mm) in from
the raw edge.

15 Lay the front cover facedown
on top of the lining/flaps,
right sides together. Stitch around
the perimeter, taking care to leave
a 4" (10 cm) gap at the bottom
for turning. Clip the corners and
turn right-side out. Use a tool like
a knitting needle to push out the
corners (take care to avoid poking
through the fabric). Press well,
making sure that the edges of the
gap are folded so that they are in line
with your seam.

16 Topstitch carefully around the
perimeter, with the elastic on
top so you're aware of its location.
When you get to the part of the
cover where the elastic is attached,
stretch it out of the way so you don't
stitch over it. Insert your journal or
sketchbook and you are done. 🖉

Visit **CANDY GLENDENING'S** website at
candiedfabrics.com.

Artify the Journal

Unleash your creative muse! Whatever you love to create,
the outer panels are the place to share this with the world.
In the featured examples, I fused a piece of accent fabric
to the front and used it as an anchor for free-motion
machine sketching. I thread my machine with a very thick
(24-weight), slightly variegated thread and a very strong
needle (denim/topstitch), and I use 50-weight cotton bobbin thread (matching the main color of the top thread). I
free-motion stitch with no markings, but feel free to mark
your stitching design lightly on your journal if you wish.

Scrappy Composition Notebook Cover

by Jamie Gonce

The inspiration for this project came from wanting a gift appropriate for anyone: kindergartener, teenager, or a best friend. As long as your cover panel measures 27½" × 11" (70 × 28 cm; see figure 1 on page 18), you can adapt this to any patchwork design (stripes, squares, etc.).

Materials

For Plain Cover:

—From Fabric A, 22" × 11" (56 × 28 cm) main cover piece and 6" × 6" (15 × 15 cm) inside pocket piece

—From Fabric B, 6" × 11" (15 × 28 cm) inside front piece

—27½" × 11" (70 × 28 cm) piece of fusible interfacing

For Wonky Log Cabin Cover:

—From Fabric A, 14" × 11" (35.5 × 28 cm) back and inside back pieces

—From Fabric B, 6" × 6" (15 × 15 cm) inside pocket piece and 6" × 11" (15 × 28 cm) inside front piece

—10–20 rectangular fabric scraps in a variety of lengths and widths, roughly 1½"–3" (3.8–7.5 cm) wide by 5"–11" (12.5–28 cm) long

—27½" × 11" (70 x 28 cm) piece of fusible interfacing

Directions

Make the inside front and pocket

1 Hem the pocket by folding down ½" (1.3 cm), and then ½" (1.3 cm) again along the top. Press and sew.

2 Lay the pocket on top of the inside front with the right side of each fabric facing up and the bottom edges aligned. Pin along the right edge and baste. Set aside.

Make the cover

Note: For the plain cover, skip to Step 5.

3 To make the patchwork cover option, select a small scrap for the center. Sew a strip of fabric to 1 edge. Iron the seams away from the center. Working out from these pieces, continue rotating and sewing a scrap to the next edge until the block measures 8½" × 11" (21.5 × 28 cm).

4 With right sides together, lay the patchwork cover on top of the back cover. Align the top, bottom, and right edges. Pin and sew in place. Press open.

Attach the inside front

5 With right sides together, lay the inside front on top of the cover. Align the right edges, pin in place, and sew. Press open.

6 The total cover should now measure 27½" × 11" (70 × 28 cm; **figure 1**).

Tip

If you use an upholstery weight fabric, interfacing is not necessary for the plain cover option.

Finish the seams and edges

7 Iron the fusible interfacing to the wrong side of the cover to hide and protect the patchwork seams.

8 To stop the edges from fraying, sew close to all 4 edges of the cover with a zigzag stitch.

9 Hem the short edges by folding in ½" (1.3 cm), press, and sew.

Wrap the cover

10 Lay the panel flat with right sides up.

11 Fold the front flap in 5½" (14 cm) with right sides touching. Press and pin in place along the top and bottom edges.

12 Fold the back flap in 5" (12.5 cm) with right sides touching. Press and pin in place.

Tip

Place the notebook inside the cover to check the fit.

---

13 Backstitching on both ends, sew along the top edge with a ⅝" seam allowance and sew along the bottom edge with a ½" (1.3 cm) seam allowance. Do this for both the front and back flaps.

Tip

Check to ensure the notebook will fit snuggly; adjust the seam allowances as needed.

---

14 Turn right sides facing out and press the entire cover.

15 To insert the notebook, pull the front and back covers of the notebook together until they touch (exposing the pages), and shimmy the sewn cover on. 🍃

Visit **JAMIE GONCE'S** website at www.bricolageandbutter.com.

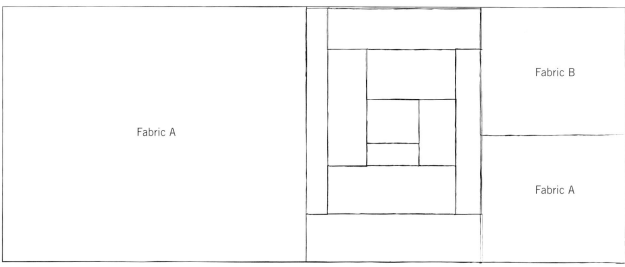

FIGURE 1

Fabric A

Fabric B

Fabric A

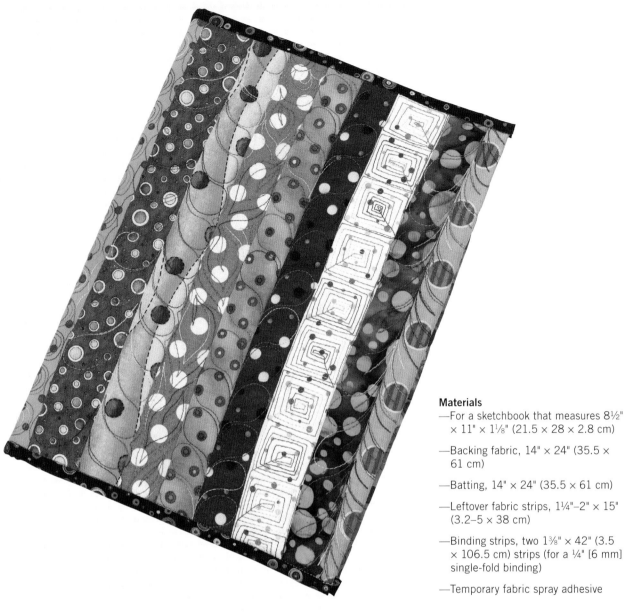

Strippy Book Cover
by Ana Buzzalino

This cover incorporates lots of leftover strips from previous projects.

Materials

—For a sketchbook that measures 8½" × 11" × 1⅛" (21.5 × 28 × 2.8 cm)

—Backing fabric, 14" × 24" (35.5 × 61 cm)

—Batting, 14" × 24" (35.5 × 61 cm)

—Leftover fabric strips, 1¼"–2" × 15" (3.2–5 × 38 cm)

—Binding strips, two 1⅜" × 42" (3.5 × 106.5 cm) strips (for a ¼" [6 mm] single-fold binding)

—Temporary fabric spray adhesive

Directions

1 Press the backing fabric and place it wrong-side up on a flat surface. Lightly spray the fabric with the adhesive and place the batting on top of the fabric.

2 Place 1 strip of fabric right-side up in the center of the batting. Place a second strip right-side down on top of the first strip and stitch the strips together using the edge of the presser foot as a guide. Press open.

Note: Piecing in this way creates great lines of stitching on the backing.

3 Continue adding strips in this manner until the foundation is covered.

4 Add extra quilting now, if you wish, and then trim the foundation to 22" × 12" (56 × 30.5 cm).

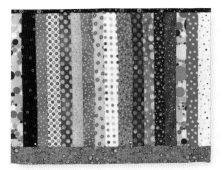

FIGURE 1

Book cover interior

5 Sew the binding pieces to the short sides first, using a ¼" (6 mm) seam allowance. Turn the binding strips to the back, fold under ¼" (6 mm), and then stitch. Trim the ends as needed.

6 Fold the short sides of the cover 2" (5 cm) to the back to form the flaps. Pin in place.

7 Turn 1 short end of the remaining binding strip 1" (2.5 cm) to the wrong side. Place the strip along the top edge on the front of the cover, right sides together, aligning the folded end of the strip with the flap's folded edge. Pin along the length of the binding strip, turning 1" (2.5 cm) under at the opposite end of the strip as well.

8 Sewing from the right side, start stitching, backstitch, and continue sewing until you reach the other end. Backstitch again.

9 Turn the binding strip to the back, fold under ¼" (6 mm), press, and sew the binding in place. Repeat with the other side (**figure 1**).

10 Place the cover on the sketchbook. Enjoy! 🖉

Visit **ANA BUZZALINO'S** website at patchesandpaint.com.

Fabric-Covered Notepads
by Megan Smith

These notepads fit the bill and allow for ample creativity. To make my notepad covers, I used 100% linen left over from a previous project along with other scrap fabric pieces. You could easily use quilt fabrics, fat quarters, fabric remnants, burlap, or even vinyl. Adding embellishments like embroidery, stenciling, notions, and stamping will bring personality to your notepad cover, so have fun with it! Be sure to write a note on the first page of the notepad; this personal touch shows care and appreciation for the recipient.

Materials

— Fabric for the front, 10" × 11" (25.5 × 28 cm) rectangle

— Fabric for the lining, 10" × 11" (25.5 × 28 cm) rectangle

— Fabric for the inside pocket, 4½" × 8" (11.5 × 20.5 cm)

— Batting, 10" × 11" (25.5 × 28 cm) rectangle

— ⅜" (1 cm) wide elastic to hold the notepad, ¼ yd (23 cm) length

— Button, ¾" to 1ʰ (2–2.8 cm) diameter

— Narrow ribbon or cording for the closure, ¼ yd (23 cm) length

— Notepad, 4" × 8" (10 × 20.5 cm; these are available at most craft stores.)

— Materials for embellishing (needle and thread, stamps and ink, stencils, etc.)

Finished Size

5" × 9" (12.5 × 23 cm)

note

* To make a cover for another size notepad, calculate the fabric and lining rectangle sizes as follows. For the width, multiply the width of the notepad by 2 and add 2" (5 cm). For the length, add 3" (7.5 cm) to the length of the notepad.

Directions

1 Embellish the right side of the front fabric rectangle with quilting, needlework, stamping, or any technique of your choice. Keep in mind the center fold and ½" (1.3 cm) seam allowance when planning your embellishment.

2 Press the pocket fabric side and bottom edges under ½" (1.3 cm). Press the top edge under in a doubled ½" (1.3 cm) hem and topstitch it in place. Position the pocket on the right side of the lining fabric, 1¼" (3.2 cm) from the left edge and 2½" (6.5 cm) from the top edge; pin it in place. Topstitch the side and bottom edges of the pocket to the lining.

3 Cut (2) 4¼" (11 cm) long strips of elastic. Pin 1 strip across the right half of the lining, 1½" (3.8 cm) from the top edge and ¾" (2 cm) from the right edge. Pin the second strip 2" (5 cm) from the bottom edge and ¾" (2 cm) from the right edge.

4 Use a wide zigzag stitch and a short stitch length to securely stitch all 4 of the elastic ends to the lining. Slide the cardboard back of the notepad through the elastic strips and make sure it fits snugly. If not, zigzag stitch again, making the opening a bit smaller. Remove the notepad and set it aside.

5 Place the embellished front right-side up on the batting. Sew the button in place through both layers, ¾" (2 cm) from the right edge and 5" (12.5 cm) from the top edge.

6 Wrap the ribbon or cording around the button and, adding 2" (5 cm) to the length for overhang, cut the ribbon. Fold it in half to make a loop, then tack the ribbon together 1" (2.5 cm) from the ends.

7 Pin the lining to the front fabric with right sides together and the batting on the bottom. Measure 5" (12.5 cm) from the top on the left edge and pin the looped ribbon between the front and lining layers with the 1" (2.5 cm) ends extending outward and the loop lying between the front fabric and lining.

8 Sew the layers together, stitching around the perimeter with a ½" (1.3 cm) seam allowance and leaving a 2" (5 cm) opening for turning. Trim the corners. Turn the notepad cover right-side out and press, pressing the opening seam allowances under. Check to see if the ribbon wraps nicely around the button and adjust if needed. Topstitch around the edges, stitching the opening closed.

Insert the notepad and enjoy! 🖋

MEGAN SMITH can be found online at hiphome.blogspot.com.

Quilted Cover
FOR YOUR SKETCHBOOK, JOURNAL, OR PLANNER
by Naomi S. Adams

I take my planner and sketchbook everywhere and always need pockets to stash pencils, pens, and the many random pieces of paper that come my way. I made myself a colorful planner cover with pockets that are perfect for holding lists and pens. Checking things off my to-do list is now much more fun! This sketchbook cover pattern will make it easy for you to whip up a few fabulous gifts for friends. They'll think of you fondly when they always have a pen handy to scribble down their thoughts or sketch out new ideas. And for a truly unique gift, use your own fabulous surface-designed fabrics.

Materials

—Journal, sketchbook, or planner (see Note)

—Fabric for main cover and cover lining, 2 rectangles 13" × 21" (33 × 53.5 cm)

—100% cotton batting, low-loft (thinner is better), 1 rectangle 13" × 21" (33 × 53.5 cm)

—Coordinating thread

—90/14 sewing machine needle

—Fabric for pocket, 1 rectangle 14" × 19" (35.5 × 48.5 cm; this is the fabric that will be most prominent on the cover. If you are auditioning a large print for the pocket, note that this piece will be folded over in half lengthwise to make a 7" × 19" [18 × 48.5 cm] rectangle.)

—Marking pencil

—Flexible tape measure (if you are covering a custom book)

note

✱ These instructions are for an 8½" × 5½" (21.5 × 14 cm) spiral-bound, 100-page sketchbook. You can adapt this pattern to cover any size journal, sketchbook, or planner. If you are covering a custom-sized book, refer to the "Custom Cover Tutorial" for instructions on how to calculate your pattern dimensions.

Directions

Prepare the main cover

1 Sandwich the batting between the main cover and cover-lining fabrics. Machine- or handquilt the main cover.

2 Using a rotary cutter, trim the main cover to 11" × 19" (28 × 48.5 cm) or the appropriate size for your custom book cover).

Attach the pocket

3 Press the pocket fabric in half lengthwise (wrong sides together) to measure 7" × 19" (18 × 48.5 cm). Topstitch ¼" (6 mm) from the folded edge (this will be the top of the pocket).

4 Position the pocket (right-side up) on the main cover (right-side up), and align the raw edges of the pocket with the bottom and side edges of the main cover. Pin in place.

5 With a marking pencil, draw the vertical stitch lines for the pen holder on the pocket as follows: Mark the first line 8½" (21.5 cm) from the right raw edge of the cover. Mark the second line 7¼" (18.5 cm) from the right raw edge of the cover. (For a custom cover, adjust these dimensions according to the directions.)

6 Straight stitch the two marked lines, starting from the top of the pocket and stitching to the bottom raw edges of the cover. Pull the starting threads to the back of the cover and bury the knots.

7 Baste the pocket to the quilted cover ⅛" (3 mm) from the edge along the sides and bottom. Remove any pins that are still in the cover.

Construct the cover flaps

8 Zigzag stitch the quilted cover fabric on all four raw edges to prevent fraying. Set your stitch width to 4 mm and your stitch length to 1 mm.

9 Press the side edges ¼" (6 mm) toward the back of the quilted cover. From the back of the cover, straight stitch ⅛" (3 mm) from the turned edge on both the right and left sides.

10 Press and pin over the top and bottom edges ¾" (2 cm) toward the back of the main cover. Topstitch

---

Custom Cover Tutorial

These instructions will help you cover any size spiral sketchbook, journal, or planner.

Main fabric height: Measure the height of your sketchbook, journal, or planner. Add 2½" (6.5 cm). This is your trimmed main fabric height after quilting. Add 2" (5 cm) to this dimension for your fabric and batting sizes before quilting.

Main fabric width: Using a flexible measuring tape, measure your sketchbook, journal, or planner from the right edge of the back cover all the way around the spine to the right edge of the front cover. Add 6½" (16.5 cm). This is your trimmed main fabric width. Add 2" (5 cm) to this dimension for your fabric and batting sizes before quilting.

Pocket fabric: The 14" (35.5 cm) raw pocket height is the perfect size to hold pens securely, so if the book you are covering is 7"–9" (18–23 cm) tall, use 14" (35.5 cm) for the raw pocket height. If your book is an alternate height, simply add 1" (2.5 cm) to the height of the book to determine your finished cover size. You can then choose a finished pocket height that appeals to you in relation to the finished cover size. Simply take your finished pocket height, add ¾" (2 cm), and multiply by 2 to calculate the raw pocket height. The pocket width is always the same as the main cover width when trimmed.

Pen holder lines: Fold the cover in half and mark vertical lines on the front half of the cover 1" (2.5 cm) and 2¼" (5.5 cm) from the left-hand side folded edge.

½" (1.3 cm) from the top and bottom edges across the entire horizontal width of the cover.

11 Fold over the side flap edges 2½" (6.5 cm) toward the cover lining. Press and pin in place. Place the book in the cover to ensure a good fit. Adjust the width of the side flaps if necessary. Check that each flap is the same width.

12 Topstitch ⅛" (3 mm) from the edge along the top and bottom of the cover. Backstitch for strength where the flap meets the cover. Bury or trim your threads. 🍃

Visit **NAOMI S. ADAMS'S** website at killerbeedesigns.com.

Journal cover interior

Journal cover exterior

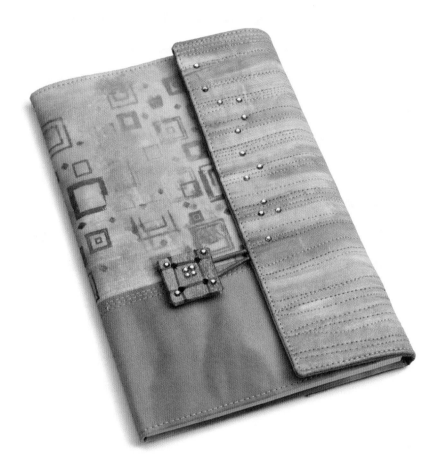

Junior Legal Pad Folio

by Diane Rusin Doran

Sometimes, it seems that lists are all that keep me on track. Here's a lovely, yet very functional, way to help stay the course, or make it as a quick gift for a special friend.

This easy fabric cover will hold a 5" × 8" (12.5 × 20.5 cm) junior-sized legal pad. You can make it as streamlined or as fancy as you wish. When open, there is a pocket for receipts or index cards on the left, while the center pocket holds the legal pad. A decorative flap holds it closed and protects the pad, while allowing space to embellish to your heart's desire.

Materials
—Fabric rectangles, one 11" × 24¼" (28 × 61.5 cm) for folio and one 8½" × 10" (21.5 × 25.5 cm) for flap, or coordinating fabrics pieced and cut to these measurements (If you plan to quilt either the folio or the flap, cut the pieces slightly larger, quilt, and then trim to sizes given.)

—Fusible heavyweight interfacing rectangles, 10½" × 12" (26.5 × 30.5 cm) for folio and 8" × 10" (20.5 × 25.5 cm) for flap

—Paper-backed fusible web, 2 strips ½" × 10¼" (1.3 × 26 cm) and 2 strips 1½" × 8" (3.8 × 20.5 cm)

—Button and 6" (15 cm) length of elastic, magnetic snap, or Velcro for closure

—5" × 8" (12.5 × 20.5 cm) legal pad

—Matching sewing thread

—Iron and ironing surface

—Sewing machine

Optional
—Choice of embellishments: stamps, beads, paint, machine embroidery, needlework

Directions

1 Iron the 10½" × 12" (26.5 × 30.5 cm) piece of fusible interfacing to the wrong side of the larger piece of fabric, centering the interfacing horizontally, and allowing 8" (20.5 cm) vertically above the interfacing and 4¼" (11 cm) below it (**figure 1**, page 25).

Note: Now is a great time to embellish the cover with sewing, embroidery, beading, or the embellishments of your choice. To determine the placement for stitching and embellishments, note that the "cover" is the upper 8" (20.5 cm) of the interfacing rectangle as oriented in figure 1. The lower 4" (10 cm) of interfacing will be the inside pocket.

2 Turn the fabric right-side up. Using the interfaced area as a guide, fold the top of the fabric down and the bottom up so that you are only seeing un-interfaced fabric (and the wrong side at that). The 11" (28 cm) long raw edges should meet or slightly overlap, and the side edges should be even. Decide upon your closure method (see the following Note) and then sew the side edges, using a ¼" (6 mm) seam allowance (**figure 2**).

Note: If you are using a magnetic snap for a closure, sew the left edge of the cover. Determine the placement for the snap and attach the snap half inside; sew the other edge. If you're using an elastic loop-and-button closure (with the front cover over the flap, as in the red sample with the gold bird), insert the elastic loop before sewing the seam.

3 Trim the corners. Place the ½" × 10¼" (1.3 × 26 cm) strips of fusible web along the raw edges that meet/overlap (place 1 strip about ¼" [6 mm] above the raw edge and the other about ¼" [6 mm] below it, making sure they're centered along the raw edge). Fuse the strips in place, but do not remove the paper backing.

4 Press the seams flat and turn the folio right-side out. Carefully square up the corners, and press the folio flat. Edgestitch close to the top and bottom edges. Reach inside the

folio, remove the paper backing from the fusible web strips, and pat the folio fabric back in place. Press the folio to fuse the edges that meet.

5 Now you're ready to make the flap, which can go over or under the front. If the flap goes over the front it's a wonderful opportunity for you to have fun with quilting, embellishing, or surface design techniques. If you're not planning to quilt the flap, center and fuse the flap interfacing to the wrong side of the flap fabric.

6 Fold the interfaced flap fabric right sides together to make a 5" × 8½" (12.5 × 21.5 cm) rectangle. Sew the short edges, using a ¼" (6 mm) seam allowance (see the following Note). Trim the corners and press the seams flat.

Note: If the flap is going to go over the front and you're planning to use a loop-and-button closure, you'll need a seam along the flap's long edge for the elastic. For the peach/yellow folio,

I quilted a 5¼" × 8½" (13.5 × 21.5 cm) piece of fabric, layered it on a second piece of fabric the same size (right sides together), and sewed them together along three edges using a ¼" (6 mm) seam allowance.

7 Fuse a 1½" × 8" (3.8 × 20.5 cm) piece of fusible web to the wrong side of the flap "backing" fabric about ¼" (6 mm) from the unsewn edge. Leave the paper backing intact. Turn the flap right-side out, pressing the edges and turning out the corners. If you're using a magnetic snap insert it now. Edgestitch close to the 3 finished edges. Pull the paper off of the fusible web and fuse the layers together. Trim the raw edge slightly with a rotary cutter. Apply the remaining 1½" × 8" (3.8 × 20.5 cm) piece of fusible web to the back of the flap, aligning the 8" (20.5 cm) edge with the raw edge of the flap.

8 Place the folio cover right-side up. On the left side of the folio, align the flap with the top edge of the

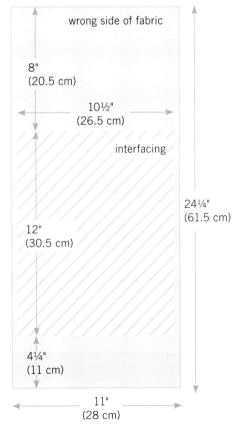

FIGURE 1

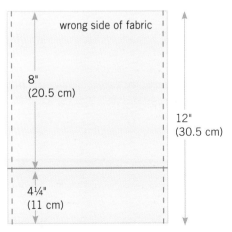

Tip
The top of the legal pad can be customized to match your cover. Apply fusible web to a 2½" × 5" (6.5 × 12.5 cm) strip of fabric. Fuse it to the top of the pad, covering the strip of paper above the perforation; then fold the fabric to the cardboard back and fuse it there.

FIGURE 2

folio, overlapping about 2" (5 cm). (On the folio, the 4" [10 cm] section of the wrapped edges will extend at the bottom.) Fuse the flap in place, and use a zigzag stitch to sew it to the folio.

9 Turn the folio over and turn up the bottom 4" (10 cm) of the folio for the pockets, making sure the bottom pocket edge is even with the bottom edge of the flap. You can also use your legal pad as a guide to determine the exact pocket depth by turning the bottom edge up over the cardboard back of the legal pad. Edgestitch the pocket in place along the side edges.

10 Insert the legal pad into the right section of the pocket. Using a needle, mark about ⅛" (3 mm) from the left side of the legal pad. Remove the legal pad. Stitch along

the marked line; then stitch ⅛" (3 mm) to the left of it to create the pocket division.

11 Edgestitch along the bottom of the left pocket. Insert the legal pad into the right pocket. Close the folio and fold the flap over. Mark the button placement on the cover or flap. Sew the button in place, making sure to sew in a shank. Bring the elastic band over the button and voilà! You have a lovely folio. 🍃

DIANE RUSIN DORAN'S widely exhibited, award-winning quilts can be seen at dianedoran.com.

Soft-Sided Portfolio
by Missy Shepler

Tuck away patterns or personal files in a desk accessory that's pretty enough to leave out in plain sight!

Materials

—⅝ yd (57 cm) of quilting-weight cotton for outer fabric

—⅝ yd (57 cm) of quilting-weight cotton for lining

—⅞ yd (80 cm) of double-sided fusible ultrafirm stabilizer (You may need to piece one 2" [5 cm] flap.)

—Round cord elastic (20" [51 cm])

—(2) ³⁄₁₆" (5 mm) grommets

—(2) ½" (1.3 cm) buttons

—Pattern paper

—3 decorative buttons (1¼" [3.2 cm], ½" [1.3 cm], and ¼" [6 mm])

Finished Size
12¼" × 9½" × 2½" (31 × 24 × 6.5 cm)

Directions

1 Refer to the illustration on page 28 to draw a full-size paper pattern. Be sure to include each set of stitch/fold lines, which are ⅛" (3 mm) wide. Cut out the pattern along the outer drawn line.

2 Press the outer and lining fabrics to remove all wrinkles.

3 Following the manufacturer's instructions, fuse the stabilizer to the wrong side of both fabrics.

4 With the outer fabric facing up, tape the paper pattern to the fused fabric panel. Use a rotary ruler or craft knife to cut along the outer pattern edges. Be sure to cut between the 3" (7.5 cm) flaps and portfolio bottom.

5 Zigzag or satin-stitch around all outer edges.

6 Straight stitch along each stitch/fold line, leaving long thread tails. Use a handsewing needle to bury the thread ends.

7 With the lining fabric facing up, use a bone folder to crease the stabilizer between the stitch/fold lines. Press the creases to set the shape.

8 Referring to the pattern for placement, insert (1) ³⁄₁₆" (5 mm) grommet in each side panel.

9 Fold the portfolio sides, flaps, and front lower flap into position. Sew a ½" (1.3 cm) button to the upper corners of the bottom flap to secure the sides and flaps in place.

10 Thread the elastic cord through the 2 largest buttons (stacked), and then insert the cord ends through the grommets. Triple-knot the cord ends to hold the cord snugly in place. Sew the ¼" (6 mm) button on top of the 2 larger buttons. 🍃

Visit **MISSY SHEPLER'S** website at missystitches.com.

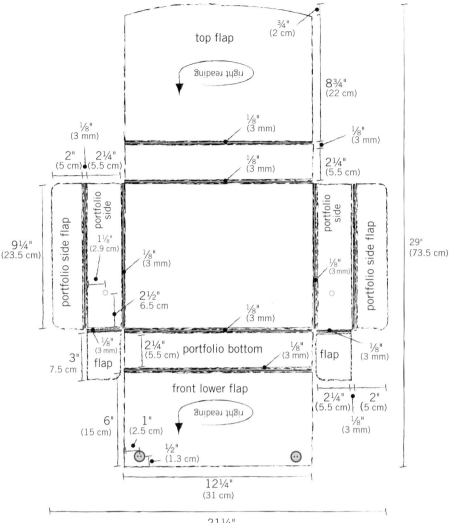

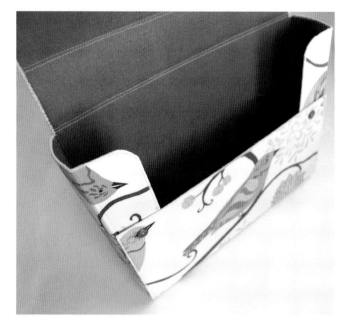

Fabric Envelope Pockets

by Missy Shepler

File personal papers, pattern pieces, and more inside a pretty fabric pocket. Need another size? Simply adjust the basic pattern.

Materials

For each file folder-sized pocket.

— 2 coordinating 12" × 20" (30.5 × 51 cm) pieces of quilting-weight cotton fabric

— (1) 12" × 9" (30.5 × 23 cm) piece of double-sided fusible ultrafirm stabilizer

— (2) 12" × 5½" (30.5 × 14 cm) pieces of fusible web

— (2) ³⁄₁₆" (5 mm) grommets

— (2) 1¼ yd (114.5 cm) of coordinating ribbon, in 2 widths

Finished Size

11½" × 9" (29 × 23 cm)

Directions

1 Carefully press both fabrics to eliminate wrinkles. Make sure both fabrics are the same size.

2 Choose 1 fabric for the pocket lining, and place it right-side down on a flat surface. Lightly mark a line 5½" (14 cm) above 1 short edge of the fabric.

3 Align 1 long edge of the stabilizer with the marked line, so that the stabilizer is in the center of the fabric. Follow the manufacturer's instructions to fuse the stabilizer to the wrong side of the lining.

4 With wrong sides facing, and taking note of the directional arrows on the pattern diagram, align the outer fabric with the lining. Fuse the outer fabric to the stabilizer.

5 Fuse the lining and outer fabric flaps together with fusible web, making (1) 12" × 20" (30.5 × 51 cm) fabric panel. If necessary, trim ⅛"–¼" (3–6 mm) from each long side to even up the edges.

6 Referring to the pattern diagram, mark and trim the curved edge of the top flap.

7 Mark and insert the eyelet grommets in the pocket back.

8 Zigzag or satin-stitch the long edge of the lower flap, leaving long thread ends.

9 Fold the lower flap up to form the pocket. Crease and press the folded edge. Starting at 1 bottom corner, zigzag or satin-stitch up the pocket side, around the top flap, and down the opposite pocket side, leaving long thread ends. Use a handsewing needle to bury the thread ends.

10 Fold the top flap into place. Layer and thread the ribbons through the grommets. 🍃

Visit **MISSY SHEPLER'S** website at missystitches.com.

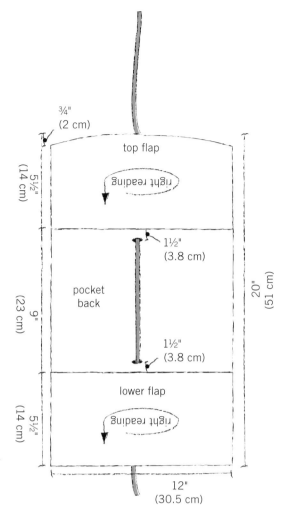

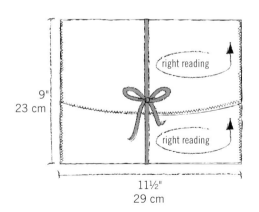

Materials

— 42" × 42" (106.5 × 106.5 cm) piece of canvas duck fabric

— Plastic sheeting or newspaper to protect your work surface

— Fabric paints in red, blue, yellow, black, and white

— 2–3 inexpensive paintbrushes or foam brushes

— Spray bottle filled with water

— Quilting mat, rotary cutter, quilting ruler

— Container of water for dipping paintbrush

— Straight pins

— Stencils, stamps with bold designs, or Thermofax screens of choice for printing on your fabric

— Sewing machine with zigzag capabilities

— Two 10" × 12" (25.5 × 30.5 cm) pieces of heavyweight stabilizer such as Peltex or fast2fuse

— Black thread

— White craft glue such as Sobo or Aleene's Tacky Glue

Directions

Painting the canvas

1 Prepare your work surface with plastic sheeting or newspaper and lay the canvas flat on top.

2 Lightly mist the canvas all over with the spray bottle filled with water. You do not want to soak the canvas but simply get it slightly damp so that the fabric paints will move and swirl together as you paint.

3 Begin painting your entire fabric. Paint freely and add splashes of color here and there. For instance, add strokes of red in one area and overlap parts with blue to create various shades of purple.

Note: You may need to spray the fabric once in a while to keep it slightly damp so that the paint will continue to move.

Decorative Fabric Portfolio

by Pokey Bolton

Do you remember going back-to-school shopping as a kid and how important it was to get the perfect set of colorful folders so you would be the envy of all of your friends? Okay, maybe I was just a school supplies geek, but now that we're adults, wouldn't it be fun to gift someone with a festive, handmade portfolio? You can adapt your fabric portfolio for a friend who is a business executive wanting to add a little flair to her office, or give it to an artist to tote art supplies in while she is in the field. In our office, we agree that an attractive folder for storing important paperwork would be a cheerful addition to our home office décor.

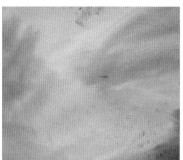

FIGURE 1

FIGURE 2

FIGURE 3

4 When painted to your liking, allow the canvas to dry thoroughly (**figure 1**).

Adding imagery

5 Now you can add imagery and interest to your large sheet of canvas by stamping with found objects or stamps with bold designs, or by using stencils or Thermofax screens with fabric paint. Overlap imagery to achieve more of a graffiti look (**figure 2**).

6 Allow the canvas to dry thoroughly.

Creating the cover

7 With your rotary cutter, cut the canvas in half. You now have two 21" × 42" (53.5 × 106.5 cm) sheets of canvas.

8 Take one piece of the canvas and set it aside; you will use this for the interior of the folder. Cut the other sheet of canvas into 2½" (6.5 cm) wide strips.

9 Arrange the strips on your work surface so that contrasting strips are adjacent, and then piece the first 2 strips together, sewing with a ¼" (6 mm) seam (**figure 3**).

10 Press the seam open on the back, using the cotton setting on your iron.

11 Add each successive strip to your pieced fabric, pressing as you go, until all strips are joined and all seams are ironed open and flat.

12 Place your newly pieced canvas on your quilting mat so that the sewing lines lie horizontally. With your rotary cutter and ruler, again cut at 2½" (6.5 cm) intervals until the whole sheet is cut (**figure 4**).

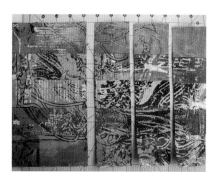

FIGURE 4

FIGURE 5

FIGURE 6

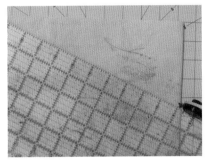

FIGURE 7

13 Repeat Steps 3–5. Do not worry if your seams don't match up exactly; mine didn't, and I think the mismatched seams add a little character (**figure 5**).

14 Using your rotary cutter, mat, and ruler, trim your pieced canvas to 20½" × 12" (52 × 30.5 cm). Save the excess pieces for another quilting project. (You've put too much work into creating this beautiful fabric to throw it away!)

15 Take your fabric folder cover to your sewing machine and, with black thread, zigzag stitch along the seams as I have begun to do in **figure 6**.

The interior

16 Take the 21" × 42" (53.5 × 106.5 cm) sheet of canvas that you previously set aside and find an area that you would like to use for the background of the interior of your folder. Rotary cut this piece to 20½" × 12" (52 × 30.5 cm) and set aside.

17 For the larger pocket, cut another piece of your fabric to 20½" × 9½" (52 × 24 cm). Fold it in half and mark a dot 4½" (11.5 cm) up from the bottom on the folded side. Take your ruler and from that mark, rotary cut to the top left corner to create an angled line. Unfold and set aside (**figure 7**).

18 Cut another piece of canvas 4½" × 20½" (11.5 × 52 cm) for the smaller pocket and set aside.

19 For the 2 business card–sized pockets, cut 2 pieces of canvas 4" × 3" (10 × 7.5 cm). Set aside.

Assembling your fabric portfolio

20 Pin your business card–sized sheets of canvas to the smaller pocket so that each is in the middle of a side. Zigzag stitch each pocket in place by stitching the 2 sides and the bottom.

21 Align 2 sheets of your heavyweight stabilizer side by side with a ¼" (6 mm) space in between. Fuse the strip-pieced cover on top. Flip it over and fuse the interior sheet (20½" × 12" [52 × 30.5 cm]) onto the back. Set aside.

22 Take the larger (angled) pocket and, using black thread, zigzag stitch all the way across the angled top. Set aside.

23 Zigzag stitch along the top of the smaller pocket.

24 Align and pin the larger pocket to the inside of the fabric folder cover.

25 Align and pin the smaller pocket on top of the larger (angled) pocket. Now all 3 layers (cover, angled pocket, and smaller pocket) should be pinned together.

26 Set your sewing machine to a wider zigzag and stitch around the perimeter of the folder, making sure to catch the sides and bottom of the pockets as you go. I recommend zigzag stitching twice around so that the pockets are more secure.

Voila! You now have a beautiful fabric portfolio to give to someone special. If you're feeling extra thoughtful, you could fill it with art supplies such as artist pens, moleskin notebooks, decorative papers, threads, and other tools so that when they open it, they find an extra special treat! 🌿

POKEY BOLTON can be found online at pokeysponderings.com.

E-Ticket Wallet

Kevin Kosbab

Travel in style with a wool felt wallet perfect for keeping your ticket and identification close at hand. The airplane appliqué and contrast topstitching combined with the inside pockets make it equally useful and stylish.

Materials

—⅓ yd (30.5 cm) (or ½ yd [45.5 cm] to allow more for error) of wool felt in main color

—2" × 2" (5 × 5 cm) piece of contrasting wool felt for airplane

—⅓ yd (30.5 cm) of medium- to heavyweight fusible interfacing (I used Pellon Craft Fuse 808.)

—Rayon embroidery thread to match main color felt

—All-purpose thread to match contrasting felt

—All-purpose thread to match main color felt

—Embroidery floss to match contrasting felt

—Embroidery needle

—E-Ticket template on page 37

—Tailor's chalk pencil

—Clear acrylic ruler with 60° markings

—Rotary cutter and self-healing mat

—¼" (6 mm) quilting foot (optional)

Finished Size
Closed: 5" × 10" (12.5 × 25.5 cm)

note

* Thread matching the felt can be used in the bobbin for all steps except the outer-edge topstitching (Step 10) if the tension is correctly set. Set the stitch length to 3 cm. A narrow-edge presser foot (such as the Pfaff Narrow Edge Foot) has a blade that can run right against the felt, making it easy to sew straight lines of topstitching ⅛" (3 mm) from the edge. A ¼" (6 mm) quilting foot can also be used, but does not have the benefit of the blade to run along the edge of the felt. If you don't have access to these presser feet, try using a ruler to draw a guideline on the fabric with tailor's chalk, then sew on the line. Go slowly to ensure straight, even stitching.

Cut Out Fabric

1 Cut 2 squares measuring 10" × 10" (25.5 × 25.5 cm) from the main color felt. Cut the following pockets from the main color felt: A rectangle measuring 9" (23 cm) long × 4½" (11.5 cm) wide (ticket pocket), a rectangle measuring 5¼" (13.5 cm) long × 3¾" (9.5 cm) wide (passport pocket), and a rectangle measuring 3¾" (9.5 cm) long × 2½" (6.5 cm)

wide (card pocket). Pin the E-Ticket template to the contrast felt and cut 1. Cut a 9½" × 9½" (24 × 24 cm) square from the interfacing.

2 Cut across one short end of each pocket piece at a 60-degree angle by placing the acrylic ruler over the felt, lining up the top of the 60-degree angle line with one corner of the short end. Mark the felt at the top and bottom of the 60-degree angle line with a fabric chalk pencil, then, using the edge of the ruler as a guide, draw a diagonal line between the two marks, extending the line at the same angle to reach the edge of the felt if necessary. Cut along the line.

3 Find the center of the bottom edge of one of the 10" × 10" (25.5 × 25.5 cm) felt squares (5" [12.5 cm] in from either side); mark a point 2¼" (5.5 cm) up from the bottom edge at the center. Use the acrylic ruler to find a 60-degree angle, as in Step 2, that runs from the bottom edge to the left of the marked point, right through the marked point. Use the edge of the ruler as a guide and draw a line, following the 60-degree angle, from the bottom edge, through the marked point, and up to the top right edge of the felt (see rotated template on page 36). Mark a point on this line that is 2¼" (5.5 cm) down from the top edge of the square (to find this point, place the ruler over the felt at a straight up-and-down angle, then move the ruler until you find the point on the diagonal line that is 2¼" [5.5 cm] from the top edge).

Assemble Wallet

4 Using the rayon embroidery thread, topstitch along the diagonal line from the top marked point to the bottom edge. If you're using fine thread, sew with a reinforced (stretch) straight stitch to make a heavier line. Then sew another parallel line of topstitching, ⅛" (3 mm) to the left of the first line, and another ⅛ " (3 mm) to the right of it. To guide the secondary rows of stitching, use a ¼" (6 mm) quilting foot: the inside edge of the toe is usually ⅛" (3 mm) from the needle position. (If you don't have a quilter's foot, simply draw guidelines on the felt with a fabric chalk pencil at the indicated

measurements. Be sure to follow the same angle all the way along the line so that the topstitched lines are even and parallel.)

5 Referring to the template on page 36, pin or glue-baste the plane appliqué at the top of the parallel lines of stitching, then whipstitch (see Sewing Basics, page 46) it in place using one strand of the embroidery floss.

6 Following the manufacturer's instructions, fuse the interfacing centered on the wrong side of the embellished felt square.

7 Referring to **figure 1** below, find and mark the center line with a ruler and fabric chalk pencil, then place the pockets on the remaining 10" × 10" (25.5 × 25.5 cm) square and pin in place. Using the contrasting-color sewing thread, topstitch around three sides of each pocket about ⅛" (3 mm) from the edge, pivoting at each corner for a continuous stitch line (rather than raising the needle) and leaving the angled side open. Backstitch (see Sewing Basics) when

starting and ending each pocket (for extra security, pull the top thread to the back and knot it with the bobbin thread).

8 Place the 10" × 10" (25.5 × 25.5 cm) squares wrong sides together and topstitch along the vertical center line using the matching sewing thread.

9 Trim any edges on which the layers aren't even, if necessary. Round each corner by using a nickel or other small round object as a guide placed at the corner, and then use a tailor's chalk pencil to draw the curve. Cut along the marked lines at the corners for clean, rounded edges.

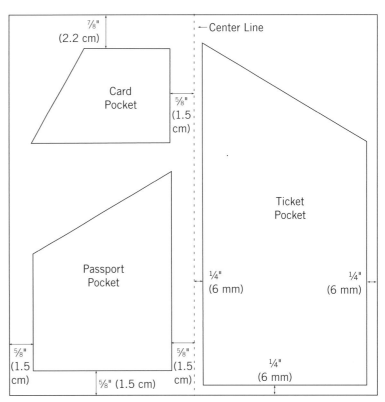

FIGURE 1

10 Using the contrasting-color sewing thread and with the outside of the wallet (embellished with the airplane) facing, start along the bottom edge, just to the left of the center line, and topstitch around the perimeter, about ⅛" (3 mm) from the edge. Pivot gradually at the corners, using four or five stitches to follow the curve of the corner. Backstitch when you reach the point where the stitching started.

11 Fold the wallet closed along the center line of stitching. Finger-press the fold or use a warm iron. 🖋

KEVIN KOSBAB is a writer, an editor, and a craft designer. Patterns for his modern quilts and sewing projects have been featured in *American Patchwork & Quilting* and *Quilts & More*. Visit his website at feeddog.net.

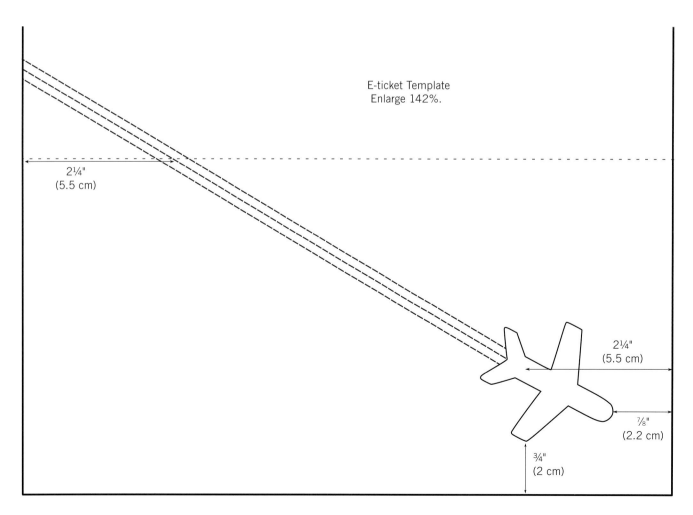

E-ticket Template
Enlarge 142%.

2¼"
(5.5 cm)

2¼"
(5.5 cm)

⅞"
(2.2 cm)

¾"
(2 cm)

Business Card Case
by Susan Brubaker Knapp

This stenciled and stitched business card case is quick and easy to make. It's also small enough to slip into a pocket and can hold a few credit cards and your driver's license if you are headed to a quilt show or concert.

Materials
—Cotton fabric (batiks work great), 10" × 10" (25.5 × 25.5 cm)

—Interfacing/stabilizer, such as Pellon 910 Sew In interfacing, 10" × 4⅞" (25.5 × 12.3 cm)

—Soft-bodied acrylic paint, such as Stewart Gill, Liquitex, Jacquard Textile Color or Lumiere, or Pebeo Setacolor (I used Lumiere.)

—Stencil brush

—Stencils or stamps

—Newspaper or other protective cover for your work surface

—Iron and ironing board

—Pressing cloth (or piece of unwanted fabric) for pressing and heat setting

—Quilting pins

—Cotton thread for construction and quilting (I used Aurifil Cotton Mako #40- and #50-weight.)

—Sewing machine with free-motion stitching capabilities

—Handsewing needle and thread

—Blunt-tipped object for pushing out corners

Directions

1 Cut 2 pieces of fabric 10" × 4⅞" (25.5 × 12.3 cm).

2 Cut 1 piece of interfacing 10" × 4⅞" (25.5 × 12.3 cm).

3 Place 1 piece of fabric right-side up on a piece of newspaper. Use fabric paint to stencil or stamp designs onto the fabric.

4 After the paint is dry, heat-set the fabric by placing a pressing cloth or piece of unwanted fabric on top and ironing.

5 Layer the pieces in the following order: interfacing, the undecorated fabric (right-side up), and then the decorated fabric (wrong-side up). Pin all the pieces together around the perimeter.

6 Stitch the 3 layers together by stitching around the perimeter using a ¼" (6 mm) seam allowance. Backstitch at the beginning and end, and leave a 2" (5 cm) opening on 1 of the short sides for turning. Clip the corners (**figure 1**, page 38).

7 Turn the card case right-side out, with the interfacing inside. Push out the corners with a blunt-tipped object. The piece should now measure 9½" × 4⅜" (24 × 11 cm).

8 Turn the raw edges under at the opening and press. Handstitch the opening closed.

9 Drop your feed dogs, and put a free-motion quilting or embroidery foot on your machine. Free-motion quilt your card case as desired. You can quilt around the stenciled design or stitch an overall pattern.

10 Fold the card case in half, right-side out, so the piece measures 4¾" × 4⅜" (12 × 11 cm). Press.

11 Open up the piece, and fold the top and bottom edges down about 2⅛" (5.5 cm) to form the 2 inside pockets (**figure 2**). Pin the folds in place from the outside of the card holder.

12 From the outside, stitch around the perimeter of the card holder about ⅛" (3 mm) from the edge. This will secure the pockets down on the back (**figure 3**). 🍃

Visit **SUSAN BRUBAKER KNAPP'S** website at bluemoonriver.com.

wrong side of fabric

FIGURE 1

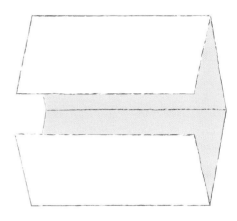

FIGURE 2

FIGURE 3

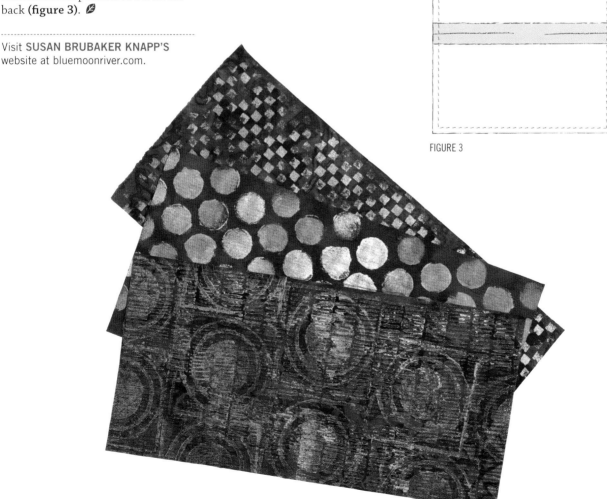

Materials
—Scraps of fabric, stamped and embellished to suit your whim (see Step 1.)

—Embellishments: ribbon, trims, fibers, buttons, charms, beads, etc., for front cover

—Double-sided, stiff, fusible interfacing, two 5" × 5" (12.5 × 12.5 cm) squares (I like fast2fuse.)

—Fabric for back, 5" × 5" (12.5 × 12.5 cm)

—Fabric for lining, 5" × 10½" (12.5 × 26.5 cm)

—4 of pattern piece A in coordinating fabrics for CD sleeve flaps

—Fusible web (I like HeatnBond Lite.)

—Ironing board and iron

—Parchment paper or a Teflon sheet, to protect ironing board

—Dimensional paint

Optional
—Lumiere paints

—Dye-na-Flow paints

—Cording

—Label holder

—Purchased appliqués

Directions

1 Compose the front cover using one of the interfacing squares as a base; stitch and fuse fabric scraps into place, being careful to protect your ironing board. (For design ideas, see "Mix & Match sidebar" on page 40) When your design is complete, trim your composition even with the interfacing square.

2 Fuse the back fabric to the second interfacing square.

3 To make a ribbon closure, fold a 10" (25.5 cm) length of ribbon in half, center the folded edge on the unfinished side of the back about ¼" (6 mm) from the raw edge, and pin in place. (The loose ends of the ribbon should extend beyond the piece.) Or use one 6" (15 cm) length of decorative fiber or cording and position in place as for ribbon.

4 Position the front and back covers with right sides down on the ironing board, leaving a ¼" (6 mm) gap between the 2 covers. Check to make sure the placement is correct. Place the lining fabric, right-side up, on top of the covers, carefully aligning the outside edges. Fuse the lining into place.

Embellished CD Covers
by Karen Fricke

My computer emits a satisfied hum when I slide in a blank CD and click the "burn" button. This miracle of modern technology has made sharing photos easy, but the plain plastic cases used to store CDs aren't very festive. This project is a fun way to turn a CD of favorite photos or a homemade family movie into a modern-day "brag book," worthy of the most special people on your gift list.

5 Use ½"–1" (1.3–2.5 cm) wide ribbon, trim, or a scrap of fabric to cover the gap along the binding edge and stitch in place.

6 Free-motion quilt the layers together.

7 To make a sleeve flap, place 2 pattern A fabrics with right sides together and stitch a ¼" (6 mm) seam allowance along the curved edge. Trim, turn, and press. Do likewise for the second sleeve flap.

8 Position the sleeve flaps so the curved edges overlap and the openings face the center. The right angles of the sleeve flaps should be even with the corners of the inside back. Pin in place and stitch ⅛" (3 mm) around all 4 edges of the CD cover, catching the sleeve flaps and the ribbon or cording tie.

9 Finish the raw edges by sealing them with a line of dimensional paint. When the paint is dry, add sparkle by buffing on a small amount of metallic paint, such as Lumiere. Or, zigzag the raw edges, catching funky fibers in the stitches.

10 Attach a button to the front cover. Tie the ribbons or wrap the cording around the button. If you like, add beads and charms to the end of the cord. If desired, attach additional embellishments to the cover, such as beads, buttons, hot-fix crystals, charms, trinkets, paper— anything. 🖋

KAREN FRICKE'S work has been featured in numerous publications. See more at karenfrickequilts.com.

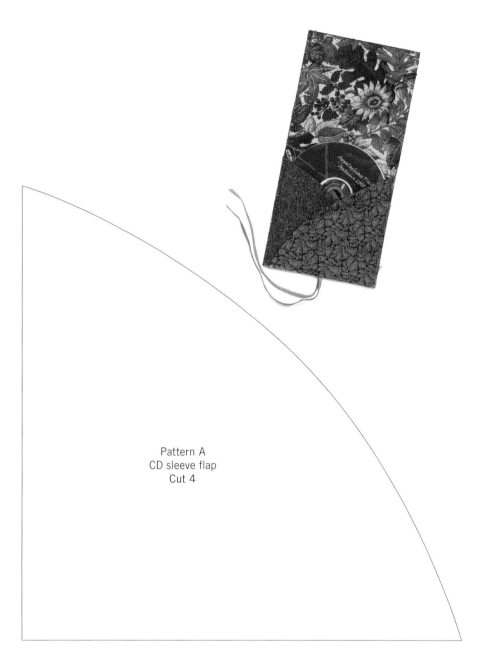

Pattern A
CD sleeve flap
Cut 4

Tips

Avoid using metallic thread, as it can scratch the CD.

Find great directions for making your own cording and tassels in Rosemary Eichorn's book, *The Art of Fabric Collage.*

These cases are also a creative way to house special collections of music. Make one for your workout tunes, another for your commute, each with themed prints and embellishments.

Mix & Match Design Ideas for the Front Cover

✳ Piece coordinating scraps together or use leftovers from other projects.

✳ Use interesting raw selvedge as a trim.

✳ Using fabric paint, stamp a decorative frame onto your fabric. Dry and heat-set, according to the manufacturer's instructions. Back this fabric with fusible web and trim it. Use it to frame a photo printed onto paper or a scrap of novelty print; fuse and stitch in place.

✳ Back novelty print motifs with fusible web and trim. Fuse in place and stitch close to the edge.

✳ Use holiday or seasonal rubber stamps and fabric paint, such as Dye-na-Flow, to decorate plain fabric.

✳ Use a narrow zigzag stitch and join lengths of ribbon together to use as you would fabric.

✳ Use decorative machine or hand embroidery stitches and interesting threads to embellish fabrics.

✳ Stitch on a label holder, the kind used for paper crafts, to identify the CD contents.

✳ Add purchased appliqués and stitch or fuse in place.

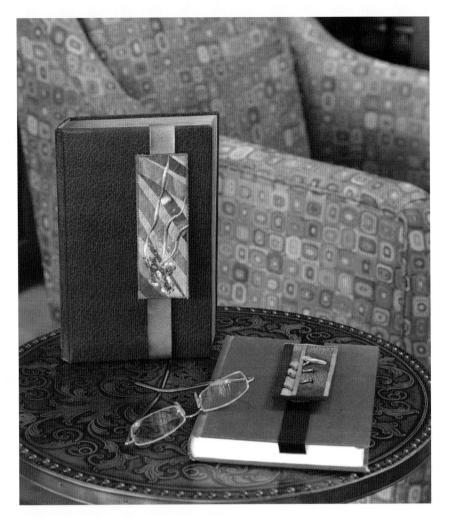

Materials

For one bookmark

—Timtex or other stiff interfacing, 2" × 6" (5 × 15 cm) rectangle

—2 fabric rectangles, each 2" × 6" (5 × 15 cm)

—2 fusible web rectangles, each 2" × 6" (5 × 15 cm)

—⅞" (2.2 cm) wide grosgrain ribbon, 19" (48.5 cm) length (I painted white ribbon. See "The Perfect Color.")

—¾" (2 cm) wide Velcro, 6" (15 cm) length

—White craft glue or glue stick

—Beads and other embellishments as desired

—Sewing machine

Optional

—Fabric paint or narrow binding

—Large fabric scraps

—Batting

note

* The design of this bookmark is such that the ribbon will extend around your book and affix to the Velcro on the back of the bookmark. Before turning/stitching the ribbon end and adding the Velcro, take a moment to determine on which side of the ribbon you should affix the Velcro.

Adjustable Fabric Boomarks

by Diane Rusin Doran

These bookmarks are an easy and elegant way to give a small gift or enhance the gift of a special book. You could personalize the bookmark by using a photo transfer of the recipient as the artwork or by matching the color of the artwork to the color of the book cover. Another option might be to use the theme of the book as a starting point for your design.

If you've made fiber ATCs (artist trading cards) or fiber postcards, the construction of this project will be a snap. The bookmark can be made with as much or as little quilting as you desire, as the small area does not require quilting for structural reasons. The materials and directions are for a 2" × 6" (5 × 15 cm) bookmark, but you can easily vary this size to suit your own design.

The Perfect Color

Both grosgrain ribbon and Velcro are manufactured in many colors. But what if you just can't find the color you want? In my samples, I simply used fabric paint on white ribbon and Velcro to customize the color to match my artwork. Spritz the ribbon or Velcro with water, apply a fluid fabric paint, such as Dye-na-Flow or Dr. Ph. Martin's, and allow to dry. The hook side of the Velcro is somewhat stiff and the looped side quite dense, so liquid fabric paint works best.

Directions

1 Apply fusible web to the wrong side of each fabric rectangle, following the manufacturer's instructions.

2 Center and glue 1 end of the ribbon to the interfacing rectangle, overlapping a short edge 1" (2.5 cm). This side will be the back of the bookmark.

3 Fuse a fabric rectangle to the back of the bookmark, covering the end of the ribbon.

4 Center the loop side of the Velcro strip lengthwise down the back of the bookmark. Sew it in place, stitching close to all edges of the Velcro.

5 Fuse the remaining fabric rectangle to the front of the bookmark.

6 Finish the edges as desired. This can be as simple as straight stitching around all edges, then covering the raw edges with paint, or you can satin-stitch or zigzag around all 4 sides. Another option is to apply a narrow binding.

7 Turn the raw edge of the grosgrain ribbon under about ¼" (6 mm), and then turn it 1" (2.5 cm); edgestitch in place. Cut a 1" (2.5 cm) piece from the hooked side of the Velcro strip and sew it to the turned-under end of the ribbon. 🖋

DIANE RUSIN DORAN'S widely exhibited, award-winning quilts can be seen at dianedoran.com.

Quilted Bookmarks

To make a bookmark with a quilted front, cut the fabric and batting each 3" × 7" (7.5 × 18 cm). Quilt the pieces together, and then trim to 2" × 6" (5 × 15 cm). If you're making multiple quilted bookmarks, rather than quilting each piece individually, layer a large square of fabric on top of a matching batting square and quilt. It's easier to stitch on the large size, and faster for cutting multiple fronts.

When I make a quilt, I quilt a few inches past the intended finished edge, then trim the excess prior to binding. These quilted scraps can be used for bookmark fronts. Add a few embellishments, cut to size, and then construct a bookmark using your quilted and embellished piece in place of the plain front. Samples you've made while trying out a new technique are another great source of design inspiration—the purple/turquoise/green bookmark was created from a long-forgotten experiment.

Sewing Basics
A quick reference guide to basic tools, techniques, and terms

For the projects in this issue (unless otherwise indicated):

* When piecing: Use ¼" (6 mm) seam allowances. Stitch with the right sides together. After stitching a seam, press it to set the seam; then open the fabrics and press the seam allowance toward the darker fabric.

* Yardages are based upon 44" (112 cm) wide fabric.

Sewing Kit

The following items are essential for your sewing kit. Make sure you have these tools on hand before starting any of the projects:

* **ACRYLIC RULER** This is a clear flat ruler, with a measuring grid at least 2" × 18" (5 × 45.5 cm). A rigid acrylic (quilter's) ruler should be used when working with a rotary cutter. You should have a variety of rulers in different shapes and sizes.

* **BATTING** 100% cotton, 100% wool, plus bamboo, silk, and blends.

* **BONE FOLDER** Allows you to make non-permanent creases in fabric, paper, and other materials.

* **CRAFT SCISSORS** To use when cutting out paper patterns.

* **EMBROIDERY SCISSORS** These small scissors are used to trim off threads, clip corners, and do other intricate cutting work.

* **FABRIC** Commercial prints, hand-dyes, cottons, upholstery, silks, wools; the greater the variety of types, colors, designs, and textures, the better.

* **FABRIC MARKING PENS/PENCILS + TAILOR'S CHALK** Available in several colors for use on light and dark fabrics; use to trace patterns and pattern markings onto your fabric. Tailor's chalk is available in triangular pieces, rollers, and pencils. Some forms (such as powdered) can simply be brushed away; refer to the manufacturer's instructions for the recommended removal method for your chosen marking tool.

* **FREE-MOTION OR DARNING FOOT** Used to free-motion quilt.

* **FUSIBLE WEB** Used to fuse fabrics together. There are a variety of products on the market.

* **GLUE** Glue stick, fabric glue, and all-purpose glue.

* **HANDSEWING + EMBROIDERY NEEDLES** Keep an assortment of sewing and embroidery needles in different sizes, from fine to sturdy.

* **IRON, IRONING BOARD + PRESS CLOTHS** An iron is an essential tool when sewing. Use cotton muslin or silk organza as a press cloth to protect delicate fabric surfaces from direct heat. Use a Teflon sheet or parchment paper to protect your iron and ironing board when working with fusible web.

* **MEASURING TAPE** Make sure it's at least 60" (152.5 cm) long and retractable.

* **NEEDLE THREADER** An inexpensive aid to make threading the eye of the needle super fast.

* **PINKING SHEARS** These scissors with notched teeth leave a zigzag edge on the cut cloth to prevent fraying.

* **POINT TURNER** A blunt, pointed tool that helps push out the corners of a project and/or smooth seams. A knitting needle or chopstick may also be used.

* **ROTARY CUTTER + SELF-HEALING MAT** Useful for cutting out fabric quickly. Always use a mat to protect the blade and your work surface (a rigid acrylic ruler should be used with a rotary cutter to make straight cuts).

* **SAFTEY PINS** Always have a bunch on hand.

* **SCISSORS** Heavy-duty shears reserved for fabric only; a pair of small, sharp embroidery scissors; thread snips; a pair of all-purpose scissors; pinking shears.

* **SEAM RIPPER** Handy for quickly ripping out stitches.

* **SEWING MACHINE** With free-motion capabilities.

* **STRAIGHT PINS + PINCUSHION** Always keep lots of pins nearby.

* **TEMPLATE SUPPLIES** Keep freezer paper or other large paper (such as parchment paper) on hand for tracing the templates you intend to use. Regular office paper may be used for templates that will fit. You should also have card stock or plastic if you wish to make permanent templates that can be reused.

* **THIMBLE** Your fingers and thumbs will thank you.

* **THREAD** All types, including hand and machine thread for stitching and quilting; variegated; metallic; 100% cotton; monofilament.

* **ZIPPER FOOT** An accessory foot for your machine with a narrow profile that can be positioned to sew close to the zipper teeth. A zipper foot is adjustable so the foot can be moved to either side of the needle.

Glossary of Sewing Terms and Techniques

BACKSTITCH Stitching in reverse for a short distance at the beginning and end of a seam line to secure the stitches. Most machines have a button or knob for this function (also called backtack).

BASTING Using long, loose stitches to hold something in place temporarily. To baste by machine, use the longest straight stitch length available on your machine. To baste by hand, use stitches at least ¼" (6 mm) long. Use a contrasting thread to make the stitches easier to spot for removal.

BIAS The direction across a fabric that is located at a 45-degree angle from the lengthwise or crosswise grain. The bias has high stretch and a very fluid drape.

BIAS TAPE Made from fabric strips cut on a 45-degree angle to the grainline, the bias cut creates an edging fabric that will stretch to enclose smooth or curved edges. You can buy bias tape ready-made or make your own.

CLIPPING CURVES Involves cutting tiny slits or triangles into the seam allowance of curved edges so the seam will lie flat when turned right-side out. Cut slits along concave curves and triangles (with points toward the seam line) along a convex curve. Be careful not to clip into the stitches.

CLIP THE CORNERS Clipping the corners of a project reduces bulk and allows for crisper corners in the finished project. To clip a corner, cut off a triangle-shaped piece of fabric across the seam allowances at the corner. Cut close to the seam line but be careful not to cut through the stitches.

DART This stitched triangular fold is used to give shape and form to the fabric to fit body curves.

EDGESTITCH A row of topstitching placed very close (1/16"–1/8" [2–3 mm]) to an edge or an existing seam line.

FABRIC GRAIN The grain is created in a woven fabric by the threads that travel lengthwise and crosswise. The lengthwise grain runs parallel to the selvedges; the crosswise grain should always be perpendicular to the lengthwise threads. If the grains aren't completely straight and perpendicular, grasp the fabric at diagonally opposite corners and pull gently to restore the grain. In knit fabrics, the lengthwise grain runs along the wales (ribs), parallel to the selvedges, with the crosswise grain running along the courses (perpendicular to the wales).

FINGER-PRESS Pressing a fold or crease with your fingers as opposed to using an iron.

FUSSY-CUT Cutting a specific motif from a commercial or hand-printed fabric. Generally used to center a motif in a patchwork pattern or to feature a specific motif in an appliqué design. Use a clear acrylic ruler or template plastic to isolate the selected motif and ensure that it will fit within the desired size, including seam allowances.

GRAINLINE A pattern marking showing the direction of the grain. Make sure the grainline marked on the pattern runs parallel to the lengthwise grain of your fabric, unless the grainline is specifically marked as crosswise or bias.

INTERFACING Material used to stabilize or reinforce fabrics. Fusible interfacing has an adhesive coating on one side that adheres to fabric when ironed.

LINING The inner fabric of a garment or bag, used to create a finished interior that covers the raw edges of the seams.

MITER Joining a seam or fold at an angle that bisects the project corner. Most common is a 45-degree angle, like a picture frame, but shapes other than squares or rectangles will have miters with different angles.

OVERCAST STITCH A machine stitch that wraps around the fabric raw edge to finish edges and prevent unraveling. Some sewing machines have several overcast stitch options; consult your sewing machine manual for information on stitch settings and the appropriate presser foot for the chosen stitch (often the standard presser foot can be used). A zigzag stitch can be used as an alternative to finish raw edges if your machine doesn't have an overcast stitch function.

PRESHRINK Many fabrics shrink when washed; you need to wash, dry, and press all your fabric before you start to sew, following the suggested cleaning method marked on the fabric bolt (keep in mind that the appropriate cleaning method may not be machine washing). Don't skip this step!

RIGHT SIDE The front side, or the side that should be on the outside of a finished garment. On a print fabric, the print will be stronger on the right side of the fabric.

RIGHT SIDES TOGETHER The right sides of two fabric layers should be facing each other.

SATIN STITCH (MACHINE) This is a smooth, completely filled column of zigzag stitches achieved by setting the stitch length short enough for complete coverage but long enough to prevent bunching and thread buildup.

SEAM ALLOWANCE The amount of fabric between the raw edge and the seam.

SELVEDGE This is the tightly woven border on the lengthwise edges of woven fabric and the finished lengthwise edges of knit fabric.

SQUARING UP After you have pieced together a fabric block or section, check to make sure the edges are straight and the measurements are correct. Use a rotary cutter and an acrylic ruler to trim the block if necessary.

STITCH IN THE DITCH Lay the quilt sandwich right-side up under the presser foot and sew along the seam line "ditch." The stitches will fall between the two fabric pieces and disappear into the seam.

TOPSTITCH Used to hold pieces firmly in place and/or to add a decorative effect, a topstitch is simply a stitch that can be seen on the outside of the garment or piece. To topstitch, make a line of stitching on the outside (right side) of the piece, usually a set distance from an existing seam.

UNDERSTITCHING A line of stitches placed on a facing (or lining), very near the facing/garment seam. Understitching is used to hold the seam allowances and facing together and to prevent the facing from rolling toward the outside of the garment.

WRONG SIDE The wrong side of the fabric is the underside, or the side that should be on the inside of a finished garment. On a print fabric, the print will be lighter or less obvious on the wrong side of the fabric.

Stitch Glossary

Backstitch

Working from right to left, bring the needle up at **1** and insert behind the starting point at **2**. Bring the needle up at **3**, repeat by inserting at **1** and bringing the needle up at a point that is a stitch length beyond **3**.

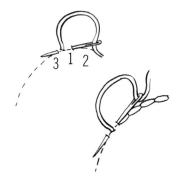

Basting Stitch

Using the longest straight stitch length on your machine, baste to temporarily hold fabric layers and seams in position for final stitching. It can also be done by hand. When basting, use a contrasting thread to make it easier to spot when you're taking it out.

Blanket Stitch

Working from left to right, bring the needle up at **1** and insert at **2**. Bring the needle back up at **3** and over the working thread. Repeat by making the next stitch in the same manner, keeping the spacing even.

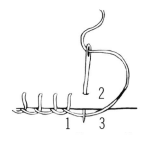

Blindstitch/Blind-Hem Stitch

Used mainly for hemming fabrics where an inconspicuous hem is difficult to achieve (this stitch is also useful for securing binding on the wrong side). Fold the hem edge back about ¼" (6 mm). Take a small stitch in the garment, picking up only a few threads of the fabric, then take the next stitch ¼" (6 mm) ahead in the hem. Continue, alternating stitches between the hem and the garment (if using for a non-hemming application, simply alternate stitches between the two fabric edges being joined).

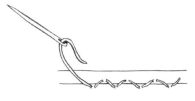

Chain Stitch

Working from top to bottom, bring the needle up at and reinsert at **1** to create a loop; do not pull the thread taut. Bring the needle back up at **2**, keeping the needle above the loop and gently pulling the needle toward you to tighten the loop flush to the fabric.

Repeat by inserting the needle at **2** to form a loop and bring the needle up at **3**. Tack the last loop down with a straight stitch.

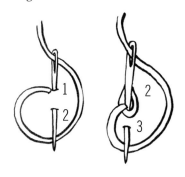

Straight Stitch + Running Stitch

Working from right to left, make a straight stitch by bringing the needle up and insert at **1**, ⅛"–¼" (3–6 mm) from the starting point. To make a line of running stitches (a row of straight stitches worked one after the other), bring the needle up at **2** and repeat.

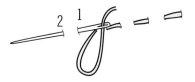

French Knot

Bring the needle up at **1** and hold the thread taut above the fabric. Point the needle toward your fingers and move the needle in a circular motion to wrap the thread around the needle once or twice. Insert the needle near **1** and hold the thread taut near the knot as you pull the needle and thread through the knot and the fabric to complete.

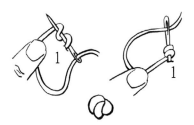

Couching

Working from right to left, use one thread, known as the couching or working thread, to tack down one or more strands of fiber, known as the couched fibers. Bring the working thread up at **1** and insert at **2**, over the fibers to tack them down, bringing the needle back up at **3**. The fibers are now encircled by the couching thread. Repeat to couch the desired length of fiber(s). This stitch may also be worked from left to right, and the spacing between the couching threads may vary for different design effects.

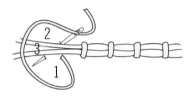

Cross-Stitch

Working from right to left, bring the needle up at **1**, insert at **2**, then bring the needle back up at **3**. Finish by inserting the needle at **4**. Repeat for the desired number of stitches.

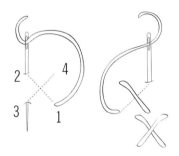

Whipstitch

Bring the needle up at **1**, insert at **2**, and bring up at **3**. These quick stitches do not have to be very tight or close together.

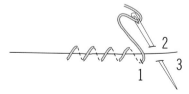

Standard Hand-Appliqué Stitch

Cut a length of thread 12"–18" (30.5–45.5 cm). Thread the newly cut end through the eye of the needle, pull this end through, and knot it. Use this technique to thread the needle and knot the thread to help keep the thread's "twist" intact and to reduce knotting. Beginning at the straightest edge of the appliqué and working from right to left, bring the needle up from the underside, through the background fabric and the very edge of the appliqué at **1**, catching only a few threads of the appliqué fabric. Pull the thread taut, then insert the needle into the background fabric at **2**, as close as possible to **1**. Bring the needle up through the background fabric at **3**, ⅛" (3 mm) beyond **2**. Continue in this manner, keeping the thread taut (do not pull it so tight that the fabric puckers) to keep the stitching as invisible as possible.

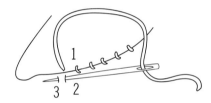

Slip Stitch

Working from right to left, join two pieces of fabric by taking a ¹⁄₁₆"–¼" (2–6 mm) long stitch into the folded edge of one piece of fabric and bringing the needle out. Insert the needle into the folded edge of the other piece of fabric, directly across from the point where the thread emerged from the previous stitch. Repeat by inserting the needle into the first piece of fabric. The thread will be almost entirely hidden inside the folds of the fabrics.

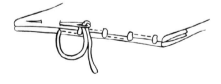

Cutting Straight Strips

Cut strips on the crosswise grain, from selvedge to selvedge. Use a rotary cutter and straightedge to obtain a straight cut. Remove the selvedges and join the strips with diagonal seams (see instructions at right).

Cutting Bias Strips

Fold one cut end of the fabric to meet one selvedge, forming a fold at a 45-degree angle to the selvedge (**1**). With the fabric placed on a self-healing mat, cut off the fold with a rotary cutter, using a straightedge as a guide to make a straight cut. With the straightedge and rotary cutter, cut strips to the appropriate width (**2**). Join the strips with diagonal seams.

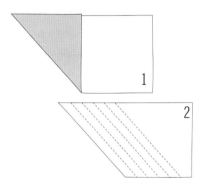

Binding with Mitered Corners

Decide whether you will use a Double-fold Binding (option A at right) or a Double-layer Binding (option B at right). *If using double-layer binding follow the alternate italicized instructions in parenthesis.*

Open the binding and press ½" (1.3 cm) to the wrong side at one short end *(refold the binding at the center crease and proceed)*. Starting with the folded-under end of the binding, place it near the center of the first edge of the project to be bound, matching the raw edges, and pin in place. Begin sewing near the center of one edge of the project, along the first crease *(at the appropriate distance from the raw edge)*, leaving several inches of the binding fabric free at the beginning. Stop sewing ¼" (6 mm) before reaching the corner, backstitch, and cut the threads. Rotate the project 90 degrees to position it for sewing the next side. Fold the binding fabric up, away from the project, at a 45-degree angle (**1**), then fold it back down along the project raw edge (**2**). This forms a miter at the corner. Stitch the second side, beginning at the project raw edge (**2**) and ending ¼" (6 mm) from the next corner, as before.

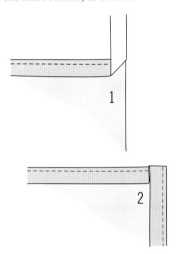

Continue as established until you have completed the last corner. Continue stitching until you are a few inches from the beginning edge of the binding fabric. Overlap the pressed beginning edge of the binding by ½" (1.3 cm) (or overlap more as necessary for security) and trim the working edge to fit. Finish sewing the binding *(opening the center fold and tucking the raw edge inside the pressed end of the binding strip)*. Refold the binding along all the creases and then fold it over the project raw edges to the back, enclosing the raw edges *(there are no creases to worry about with option B)*. The folded edge of the binding strip should just cover the stitches visible on the project back. Slip-stitch or blindstitch the binding in place, tucking in the corners to complete the miters as you go (**3**).

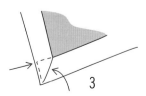

Diagonal Seams for Joining Strips

Lay two strips right sides together, at right angles. The area where the strips overlap forms a square. Sew diagonally across the square as shown above. Trim the excess fabric ¼" (6 mm) away from the seam line and press the seam allowances open. Repeat to join all the strips, forming one long fabric band.

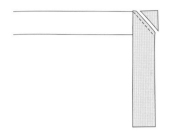

Fold Binding

A. Double-fold Binding

This option will create binding that is similar to packaged double-fold bias tape/binding. Fold the strip in half lengthwise, with wrong sides together; press. Open up the fold and then fold each long edge toward the wrong side, so that the raw edges meet in the middle (**1**). Refold the binding along the existing center crease, enclosing the raw edges (**2**), and press again.

B. Double-layer Binding

This option creates a double-thick binding with only one fold. This binding is often favored by quilters. Fold the strip in half lengthwise with wrong sides together; press.

Find popular patterns for quick and easy projects with these *Craft Tree* publications, brought to you by Interweave.

Evening Bags
ISBN 978-1-59668-764-6

Everyday Totes
ISBN 978-1-59668-774-5

Fun Home Accessories
ISBN 978-1-59668-769-1

Just for Baby
ISBN 978-1-59668-773-8

Just for Kids
ISBN 978-1-59668-772-1

Modern Sewing Projects
ISBN 978-1-59668-768-4

Notebook Covers
ISBN 978-1-59668-766-0

Patchwork Pillows
ISBN 978-1-59668-767-7

Scarves and Wraps
ISBN 978-1-59668-770-7

Teacher Gifts
ISBN 978-1-59668-765-3

Travel Accessories
ISBN 978-1-59668-771-4

Visit your favorite retailer or order online at
interweavestore.com

INTERWEAVE
interweavestore.com